Everyday Struggles

The Stories of Muslim Teens

Everyday Struggles

The Stories of Muslim Teens

A collection of short stories written by
Sumaiya Beshir and other Muslim teens

COMPILED BY SUMAIYA BESHIR

amana publications

First Edition
2004A.C./1425A.H.

Second Printing
2007A.C./1427A.H

Copyright © 2004 A.C./1425 A.H.
amana publications
10710 Tucker Street
Beltsville, MD 20705-2223 USA
Tel: (301) 595-5999
Fax: (301) 595-5888

Email: amana@igprinting.com
Website: amana-publications.com

Library of Congress Cataloging-in-Publication Data

Beshir, Sumaiya.
  Everyday struggles : the stories of Muslim teens / written and compiled
by Sumaiya Beshir.
      p. cm.
  ISBN 1-59008-030-0
  1. Group identity–United States. 2. Muslim youth–United States. I.
Title.
  HN59.2.B475 2004
  305.235'088297–dc22

                                                    2004019495

Printed in the United States of America by
International Graphics
10710 Tucker Street
Beltsville, MD 20705-2223 USA
Tel: (301) 595-5999
Fax: (301) 595-5888

E-mail: ig@igprinting.com
Website: igprinting.com

Dedication

For those who refused to allow the teenage years
to claim another young and vibrant life

For those who smile in the face of adversity
because they remember that
God tests those whom He loves

For those who pray in corridors and closets,
tucked quietly away,
because prayer is too important to be missed

For those who laugh and cry for Islam,
May every tear and chuckle be a weight
on your scale of good deeds

For those who are content with this life
but eagerly await the next

For those who speak beautiful words,
for there is no pain greater to the ears
than vulgar language.

For those who know the importance of respect,
for themselves just as much as for those around them

For those who know who their true beholder is
and seek to always please Him

Let not a day go by without Allah's remembrance
Let not the hours pass like a fleeting flock of birds
Let not the spending of your time be haphazard
For those who place their trust in God's arms
because they are stronger and gentler
than any arms on this Earth

Table of Contents

Acknowledgements

All praise is to Allah the most high, the beneficent, the merciful. I would like to express my deepest and sincerest gratitude to my mother and father for their undying support for this book. Your encouragement and inspiration made it possible. Your vision and dedication made it real. I would also like to thank Jennifer Templin for her valuable contributions. Your hard work and conviction are rare gems that I greatly cherish. To my sister, Hoda, who pulled through for me in the knick of time. To all who have contributed their time, effort and experience to this book. May Allah reward you all with the highest and finest of rewards. And to the reader, it is my sincere hope that you enjoy this book and find yourself, or at least bits and pieces of yourself, in one of the stories.

Forgotten Blessings

THEY are all around us. Some are hidden while others are so blatantly obvious you couldn't miss them with your eyes closed. But we miss them all the same. There was a time in my life when I believed I was less fortunate than others, felt that life just wasn't going my way. I fell into the bad habit of trying to count my blessings and I often noted that they were few and far between. I note now that I didn't do a very thorough job of counting, for there were a few biggies I totally missed. But of course you never know what you have until it's gone—a sad saying, and all too true.

When I was eighteen I reached the peak of my bad fortune, or so I'd thought. Everyday while getting on the public bus heading to school I'd pick out girls who were prettier than me, fairer than me, taller than me, slimmer than me. It's funny how I never seemed to notice those I had a chance of beating in my little blessings contest. If their nose was small and curved, they'd get a point, for I had a button nose. If their eyes were big and round, they were automatically winning, for my eyes were rather on the small side. If they wore sandals, I examined their toes. Short and stubby, I thought, were at least better than long and finger-like. But it didn't stop at that. At school, I envied those who got higher marks than me, though I never really put much effort into homework and assignments. I was smart and I knew it, but mere intelligence was not enough to get me by anymore, and I wasn't willing to put in an ounce of extra effort. So instead of A's I got high C's, and on the days I actually studied for tests, B's. But I envied my friends nonetheless, completely overlooking the fact that I had it in me to do as well as them, if not much better.

I had never been the athletic kind. I considered the 7-minute walk to my bus stop an exhaustive workout. And since our home was two stories high with a basement, I got my stair-master routine in naturally just by moving around the house. That was really the extent of my exercise, except for the rare soccer game my friends and I would play at a nearby park. We'd use our knapsacks as the goal posts, divide ourselves up into uneven teams of 3 and 2 (we were usually 5 altogether) and kick the ball around for a bit before one of us quickly developed painful cramps.

I never held a real job either. One by one, I watched my friends brush up their resumes as we hit grade eleven and as we entered grade 12 most of them had successfully landed jobs at the local pharmacy, coffee shop or sporting goods store. I however, continued to do menial jobs for my parent's friends; babysitting, lawn mowing, the usual. There was also the paper route I held for a year, but I never considered that a real job because I wasn't interviewed for the position. All in all, I felt I was losing on most fronts. In looks, school, sports and work I wasn't scoring too high. Or rather, as I believed at the time, I wasn't highly blessed. But at eighteen, the same year I delved so deeply into self-pitying misery, life threw me a serious curve ball. Some would call it a tragic calamity—I call it a blessing in disguise. For a girl who thought she had no blessings left to count, a whole lot were suddenly found and taken away.

It was mid June and my parents, older sister and I were heading to my sister's university awards ceremony at the university she attended in Toronto where we lived. It was a long and tedious procession. Student after smiling student bashfully walked onto stage and, grinning widely, accepted their certificate, or medal, or trophy or whatever. My sister was in the last batch of blushing second year students since our last name, Yehya, began with a Y—the cruel irony of alphabetical order. I sat sandwiched between my parents in seat 79C, glancing at my watch more often then I can remember and secretly praying that a stomach flu had exclusively struck all students with last names ending with C through Q. But no such stomach flu seemed to be in the air, or if it was, students C through Q had all faithfully taken their Pepto-Bismol before the ceremony.

"Erika Pram." The master of ceremonies had a strong and commanding voice.

"Erika is the recipient of the Margaret Jennings award for outstanding academic achievement in electrical engineering."

Beaming with joy, Erika ran up the side steps of the stage almost tripping along the way. She may be good with circuits, I smirked to myself, but she's kind of on the clumsy side.

Throughout the ceremony, I did what I could to protect my pride, which was severely wounded at this point from the sight of so many overachievers of whom I was not one. I feigned boredom, made fun of Erika and the like and tried desperately to yet again put stomach flu curses on the remainder of the alphabet, but to no avail. In the end, I watched over 200 university students celebrate their accomplishments—I considered this yet another blessing I had missed out on. 2 hours later, as James Zhong stepped onto the stage, I thanked the Lord that it was finally over, or at least that the ceremony was finally over. It was now time for refreshments in the grand hall. The crowd of proud students, parents and professors poured out of the auditorium and I soon found myself sandwiched yet again, but this time between a hungry hoard of people trying to act civilized as they approached the platter of delectable desserts. I cut myself a slice of strawberry cheesecake and garnished it with a few pieces of cantaloupe. Well, at least tonight wasn't a complete waste of time, I thought to myself, as I bit into the thick crust. Very soon I would learn how true that statement really was. For that night would be the last time my family and I would all be together.

I made my way through the bustling hall until I finally caught a glimpse of my parents standing beside another couple, laughing and talking. Great, I thought, they're mingling. As harmless as it appeared, I knew the true repercussions of mingling parents. Mingling parents meant a longer stay in this place, which meant a delayed return home, which meant I would miss Survivor. I saw my sister heading toward me then, the shiny silver medal glistening around her neck. She smiled and waved at me between the massive crowd. I pretended not to see her, pretended to be looking past her and up at the exquisite architecture of this fine academic institution, as my parents called it. My sister was the exact opposite of me in many ways. She wasn't as inherently intelligent as me and since school was a challenge for her, she found her niche in sports. In high school she played competitive soccer. I watched her from the stands. But whether it was sports or school, she always put in 110%. This had led her far in her short life, and I sorely begrudged her for it. But there was no room for the self-pitying in that grand hall, so I resorted to subtle sarcasm and secretly resenting my sister. I resented her hard work, her good grades, and the goals she scored during her soccer games. I resented the job she held as a receptionist and the dimples she had when she smiled. And that day, most of all, I resented the gleaming medal that hung around her neck. Actually, as I look back on it now, it wasn't so much my sister that I resented, it was God. I resented God for forgetting me from his blessings like an ungrateful child who resented her parents for doing what is best.

After the mingling subsided, my parents took out their trusty camera. They began snapping pictures of my sister with her shiny new hardware as I went back to the dessert table for seconds. The chocolate fudge truffle cake was particularly tasty and after only one slice I was better able to keep my boredom in check. I checked my watch as I headed back over to my parents and sister, giving in to their persistent cries for a family photo by the grand staircase. It read 8:25, I'd missed 25 precious minutes of Survivor. Just enough to erase any pleasant memory I had of that cake and thrust me back into a miserable mood. I tugged at my mother's blouse like a three year old as soon as the camera had flashed. "Can we please go now?" I whined. I wanted to at least catch the last 15 minutes of the show.

We piled into our car, my sister smiling with her polished medal dangling on her neck. Me yawning, checking my watch incessantly and asking my dad if he could please take the highway and step on it. We were at the major intersection before our street when it happened. I had begged my sister to decline my mother's invitation to the Krispy Kreme doughnut shop so I could get home in time for tribal council. My mother's happy voice drifted through the car. She was telling us about a nice professor she'd spoken with that night. She had always been a content woman even when the people around her found nothing to be thankful for. But her sweet voice was brusquely drowned out and all too quickly replaced with a terrible sound that rung painfully in my ears. Shattered glass raged in every direction and I watched in horror as my sister's new medal flew off her wilted neck and out through the broken windshield. The last thing I remember was the distant sound of a siren.

I was told my sister died on impact. My mother and father held out for a few hours but passed on shortly after being admitted into the emergency room. I was entwined in a knot of disarray, they said. It took the paramedics 2 hours to untangle me from the mess. It was a day and a half before I regained consciousness and learned the fate of my family. Every inch of my body wept for them—every inch I could still feel at least.

For the longest time I mourned my forgotten blessings. The sister I had once so bitterly resented, I now so dearly wished I could have back. I would never hold my mother's warm hands again. Never hear my father's calm whisper gently draw me from my deep dawn slumber. No longer did I yearn to be athletic, but only to feel the touch of my numb feet on the soft carpet. The accident had left me paraplegic—unable to feel anything from my waist down.

I lived with my uncle and his family in Boston after the accident. They were the closest relatives to our family both geographically and psychologically, and they took me in with open arms. They were very patient with me, and despite having 2 kids of their own, they always made sure I went to my physical therapy appointments on time. My brief loss of consciousness had stagnated some of my muscles and it took me several months to relearn simple daily acts like how to feed myself and brush my own teeth again. My uncle, being my mother's brother, bore a striking resemblance to her. As children, my sister and I often fibbed to our younger and more naïve friends that my mother and her brother were identical twins, even though we knew this was scientifically impossible. In fact, my mother was 6 years older than her brother. But now, as I looked upon his serene face, I was not comforted but deeply grieved. His existence was a constant reminder of my great loss, and sometimes at the mere sight of him, memories of my mother would come flashing back and tears would silently escape my eyes and begin to stream down my rigid face. I thought obsessively about my parents and sister. Remembered the way they talked, they way they laughed, their deep and weary sighs when I would shift into annoying mode. I called them my forgotten blessings, and with every passing day, I prayed passionately to God that if He would somehow bring them back to me, I would never take these blessings for granted again. But for all my intelligence it took me a while to figure out that there was a deeper lesson behind all this.

It wasn't until I turned twenty, two years after the accident, that it finally clicked. I had lived the last 2 years of my life chiefly inside my head. Spent my days secretly conversing with the dead and refusing to get too close to anyone lest they be taken away from me again. I revisited every memory I could recall of my past that included my family, and then, one by one, I wept fervently over the recollections I had conjured up. For months after the accident, I cried over my handicapped state. The loss of movement in my legs, I thought, was too big a loss to bear. But God does not overburden anyone beyond his capacity—I seemed to forget that for quite some time. For two years, I woke up every morning thinking today would be the day. Today my family and I would be reunited, today I would learn to walk again, today God would answer my prayers. What I didn't realize was that God had already answered my prayers and more—I was just being too stubborn to see it. I was so busy dwelling over the love I had failed to express to my parents and sister that I continued to withhold any feelings of love and appreciation from those around me. My uncle's wife was diagnosed with cancer the day I turned twenty, and for a moment, I pictured what was left of my already broken life being shattered to pieces once again. My aunt, who was in no way a blood relative of mine, had been the one who often drove me to and from the hospital for my various and numerous doctor's appointments and medical exams. And suddenly, the tables had turned and I found myself visiting her in the hospital or accompanying her on her days of intensive chemotherapy and radiation treatments. For a while, our lives were a chaotic blend of therapies and treatments, and between the two of us, we must have visited the hospital almost every second day of the week. But beneath all the hardship and ills, my aunt emerged as a very strong woman and before long I began to wish I had gotten to know her better when I had the chance. She had a cunning sense of humour and the patience of a Prophet. Through her I came to understand that the days I had spent with the dead were wasted, for there were still many living who were worth my time. Not once did I hear her utter a complaint, for unlike me, she fully understood that God does not burden anyone beyond his capacity. And for the brief period she was tested in, the cancer that plagued her made her stronger.

And so I finally learned who my forgotten blessings really were. The lesson I hadn't picked up on the first time around, had been driven home with the passing of my aunt. The day she was buried was the day I took a pledge to not allow myself to make the same unsightly mistake three times in my life. From then on, I lived in the present and tried hard to appreciate everyone and everything around me. One by one, I recalled my true forgotten blessings, and here I do not speak only of my mother or father, sister or aunt. Rather, when I speak of my forgotten blessings now, I am referring to the intelligence that God has blessed me with that remains sharp to this day. My arms, my hands, my fingers. My uncle, whose love for me is that of a caring father. My cousins who have been like beloved siblings to me and have accepted me as their older but sometimes childish sister. The doctors and nurses that patiently guide me through my many treatments, and gently push me to go just a little beyond my comfort zone. The birds that serenade me every morning, the trees that shade from the heat of the sun. But most of all, I speak here of God. For God, whom I so quickly turned my back on when the going got tough, is the one who gave me all these blessings in the first place, and reminded me of them when I had so arrogantly forgotten.

I pray for my family everyday, the living and passed alike. I turned 24 last week and have gotten rather comfortable, if not creative, in my wheelchair. I joined a local wheelchair basketball team and surprisingly found that I am much more athletic on two wheels than I ever was on my own two legs. Life still has its ups and downs, its ins and outs. At the moment, I'm kept very busy with my ongoing physical therapy, my two cousins and the correspondence courses I'm taking at Boston U. When I look back on the events of the last 6 years of my life, I'm relieved to say that they did not break me, they broke me in. God loves me, and for that very reason, He tested me with these events. The rest of my life, no matter how short or long, is my enduring chance to prove that I have learned this vital lesson once and for all, my enduring chance to recollect my forgotten blessings.

Of Malls and Movies

"Gusto Maverick commands the screen!"
"Allison Smith-Brown's best performance ever!"
"The must-see movie of the year!"

I flipped the channel only to find yet another commercial harping about how incredible Allison Smith-Brown was in "The Stock Broker". It seemed to be all anyone could talk about these days. At school the topic of conversation alternated between Gusto Maverick's cool tone of voice and Allison Smith-Brown's cool outfits. Every once in a while someone warily asked if we had any math homework. The question was always dealt with promptly though, and we would jump right back into gossiping about "The Broker", as we often called it. Even those who knew nothing about the movie pretended desperately to be in on the scoop. The phonies were often discovered however, when they slipped up and accidentally referred to the movie as "The Insurance Broker" or "The Car Dealer". I hadn't seen it myself, considering it had only been out in theatres for a week. But really, that was no excuse. In our school there was the unspoken rule that if you wanted to maintain your status in the non-loser crowd, you were to watch all movies by Allison Smith-Brown immediately upon release. I turned off the television and headed up to my room to do some homework. The movie didn't really look that interesting, I thought to myself, as a matter of fact I found Allison Smith-Brown to be genuinely annoying. As I was staring my math homework in the face and wondering how in the world I would ever solve the problem using the quadratic equation, the phone rang. It was my friend Jessica from school, and I welcomed the break, though I really hadn't done anything to deserve it. We talked for a while, mostly about The Broker and how cool it seemed. I asked her a question about the quadratic equation, she asked me if I wanted to come see the movie with a few other girls on Saturday. I hung up the phone excitedly. It was time to tackle the quadratic monster, I thought. My blank page stared back at me.

Over dinner that day, I spoke of The Broker between spoonfuls of biryani rice. It was my preparatory preamble before popping the big question of whether or not I would be allowed to go on Saturday with my friends. As we were finishing up and clearing the plates I decided I would finally take the plunge and ask my mother.

"Well, what's the movie about?" she asked thoughtfully after I had made my request.

I thought for a moment. The truth was I really didn't know anything about the movie except that Allison Smith-Brown and Gusto Maverick were in it. I didn't even know what a Stock Broker was. "I don't know," I said, "but how should I know until I see it? That's the whole point of seeing a movie isn't it, to find out what it's about? Besides all my friends are going and if I don't go, I'll look like I don't have a life." But that wasn't the end of that conversation. In fact, The Broker became a hot topic of discussion in our household for the next few days. I think I must have mentioned the name of Allison Smith-Brown more often than my own sister's name during the 2-day debate my mother and I were having. My mother's argument was that in a perfect world you could go to a movie without knowing anything about it and not be surprised by any bad scenes or bad language. But our world was far from perfect. So, I couldn't just walk naively into the theatre and hope that against all odds, through some great miracle, this movie would turn out to be fully decent. My argument: "I have no life!"

As weak as my argument may have sounded, it echoed over and over again in my mind. Every time I was told no to something, it confirmed this belief I carried around with me, whether erroneous or justified. When I wasn't allowed to go the mall with my friends, I could almost hear the words being whispered in my ears. If I couldn't buy a certain outfit, it was as if someone was muttering under their breath. "You have no life," the voice would say, and I would dismally nod my head in agreement. By the end of that week, my mother gave up and reluctantly agreed to let me go to the movie. It was obvious that her decision stemmed more out of annoyance with the topic than from conviction in the act. Nonetheless, I was happy. To me, all that mattered was that I could go—one of the first steps in acquiring a life. But I would not allow one movie to be the extent of my life. People with lives did many other things too, I was told, since I didn't know first hand. There were malls to visit and fashions to apply. And so I began my saunter down the slippery slope of "having a life". The movie was what I had expected it to be: annoying. As usual, Allison Smith-Brown trotted around like a princess lost in wild terrain, in need of a handsome savior. Gusto Maverick's tone of voice was cool for a grand total of about 10 minutes, at which point his eccentric intonation began to upset my delicate eardrums. Ironically enough, there wasn't a single bank in the entire movie. The virtually non-existent plot was reminiscent of a poorly composed story I had read in grade six once and, as my mother had predicted, some of the language used was much less than entirely appropriate.

But I put on an act. After practically begging my mother to allow me to go to this bad excuse for a movie I couldn't very well come right out and declare that it had in fact been a complete and utter waste of my time. So when the credits began to roll and the theatre lights went up, I blinked a few times and wore my finest fake smile. I nodded my head mechanically in agreement when my friends raved about how wonderfully Allison Smith-Brown had played her character and how incredible Mr. Maverick's Southern twang was. My head bobbed avidly up and down to every comment made. I didn't hear some of them and I didn't agree with most of them.

I soon learned that the practice of "having a life" wasn't as easy as I thought. You see, the process doesn't end after you see a movie. Actually, that's where it starts. Now that I'd seen the movie, I had to begin to dress like the characters in the movie, walk like the characters in the movie and talk like the characters in the movie. I had to transform myself into someone I could barely stand. I had to become Allison Smith-Brown. My friends decided that we should all go shopping together that weekend, so we could get ourselves a "decent wardrobe" as they put it. Of course they defined decent as anything that looked like what Allison Smith-Brown wore. And so, round two of the debate with my mother began. My undertaking this time was a little more difficult than the first because not only did I want her to agree to let me to go, I wanted her to help fund my little shopping trip as well. So on Monday I began what would be a weeklong campaign. At first I dropped subtle hints, made faint comments about some nice clothes I'd recently seen, mentioned in passing that I wanted to update my wardrobe just like my friends. But the subtle phase didn't last for long, maybe because I didn't execute it properly or maybe because my mother saw it coming. Either way, within a day we were once again in a dispute.

"I don't mind buying you new clothes" she would say, "But I just don't want you to buy something only because everybody else has it. Just because your friends do something, or say something or wear something doesn't mean it's right. Your friends don't set your standards and values, God does. Besides, you already have a lot of clothes, so why waste money on something you don't need anyway?"

I would look up at her then, knowing whole heartedly that she was right, but knowing also that I really wanted to go to the mall and dress like my friends. The next day, we'd be at it again. I would plead with her to let me go, ask her to support me in my important quest for a life. She would say that I had better things to do with my time than wander aimlessly around the mall for hours. Didn't I have a math test coming up, she would ask, and what about the annual science fair? But I was awfully persistent in my plea, actually it was more like stubborn, and by the fourth day my mother agreed that I could go. She even gave me some money garnished with two words of advice: shop wisely.

The mall was busy on Saturday afternoon and as we made our way from one pushy salesperson to the next, I began to feel very tired. But my friends wouldn't hear of it. They insisted that before I stepped out of the mall that day, I was to have at least bought one, there's that word again, "decent outfit". So in the end, I settled on a pair of snug black pants and sweeping polyester dress shirt. Sweeping and snug, I later learned, were just fancy ways of saying exposed and skin-tight. I have to say that even as I was trying them on in the change room I felt uncomfortable. I struggled to pull the pants up over my thighs and hips and I was almost convinced that the manufacturer had made a sweeping glitch in the sweeping blouse because of how open its neckline was. But as I opened the stall door, I could see my friend's eager eyes peering in on me, trying to catch a glimpse of what I looked like in Allison Smith-Brown's clothes. Their approving nods and flattering comments started to play on my ego until even I myself began to believe that I looked great in the outfit, as uncomfortable as it was. And so victory was declared at the cash register and my friends and I celebrated our success in finding four Allison Smith-Brown outfits in one strenuous shopping session. We must have set or broken some kind of record, we joked. If we had, I later realized that it wasn't a record I wanted to hold. But the whole bus ride home, all I could think about was my friend's favourable reactions to my outfit. I remembered the excited looks on their faces as I stepped out of my change room, fumbling with the tight pants and pulling anxiously on the sweeping shirt. I played the scene over and over again in my mind, recounted their praising remarks in elaborate detail.

My mother's reaction to the outfit, however, was not nearly as favourable. Disappointment washed over her face as I pulled the clothes out of the shopping bag and laid them down on her bed. And as I actually tried the outfit on and stood in front of her, the disappointment was quickly replaced with distress. I had taken her money but not her advice, she said, and even I knew that was true. No words were required for me to figure out that my mom thought the outfit indecent. Her definition of decency of course, unlike that of my friend's, was in no way based on Allison Smith-Brown. But still I would not admit defeat. At this point, I was fighting not out of want but out of habit, and far away from my friend's persuading cries, I too looked upon the outfit unfavourably and wondered how I had been moved to buy it. But it took a while until I would fully admit that to myself, let alone my mother. All I could think about as I stood there in my mother's room, dressed in a way that dazed me every time I looked in the mirror, was that if I had bought this outfit, then I must like it, and if I liked it, then I should defend it. And so I did. Foolishly, irrationally, hot-headedly, I defended that which I didn't even believe in.

It seemed that my mother and I were in a constant state of debate. When we finished with one issue, we'd move on to another. The issue of this week was my controversial Allison Smith-Brown wannabe outfit. I had already bought it, and now I wanted to wear it outside of my house.

"Everybody's wearing it!" I would argue.

"Just because everybody's doing anything doesn't mean its okay." she would reply, "If everybody jumped off a cliff, would you?"

"It's not the same thing" I would whine.

"But it is the same thing" she would insist "Your friends may not be jumping off the cliff just yet, but they're taking little steps toward the cliff and if you follow in their footsteps now you won't be able to stop when you reach the cliff. Don't let everybody decide what this body's going to wear."

It continued like this for a while. All week long the outfit hung dully in my closet, the price tags, still attached, bearing my mother's hope that I would soon return the outfit to the store. But by Thursday night, the price tags were cut and the hope was shattered. My mother, following another long debate, had given in.

"Wear it then," she'd said in a moment of frustration, brought about, no doubt, by my endless moaning and groaning. "But remember to keep count of the sins you'll be getting every time a boy looks at you in your tight pants and open shirt so you can make it up with good deeds after!"

I couldn't sleep very well after that. I'd almost wished she'd never given in to my steady whining, as annoying as it was. But I couldn't swallow my foolish pride just yet. So in the morning, after a night of uneasy sleep littered with a few bad dreams, I got up, got dressed Allison Smith-Brown style, and went to school. I walked slower than normal that day, the rigid pants hindering my usual pace. I stopped often to adjust the sweeping blouse, pulling the ruffled neckline up and fiddling with the drooping shoulders. The name "sweeping" was rather befitting, I thought. It should have been a broom and not a blouse. As I plodded uncomfortably through the schoolyard, I caught a glimpse of someone up ahead. The person was waving at me, hands fluttering in the air, but I couldn't for the life of me figure out who it was. The figure got nearer and I tried harder to decipher the appearance. The walk was familiar but the clothes looked very strange to me, strange and indecent. Who did I know who would dress like that? She looked terrible, I thought. I was starting to make out a few features. Her thighs bulged out, not because she was fat, but because her black pants were awfully tight. Maybe all her pants were in the wash, I thought, so she had to borrow her younger sister's. She waddled over uncomfortably now, only a few feet away from me. I did a double take as she stepped in front of me to give me a hug. "Jessica!" I screeched as I patted her back robotically. She released me from the hug and examined me curiously. "What is it?" she asked, unaware of the shock I'd just experienced. But she seemed to forget about her question when she stepped back and looked at me. "You finally wore it," she exclaimed "You look great!"

I didn't feel great. Especially after realizing that the shocking and unsightly outfit that Jessica was wearing was almost identical to the one I presently had on. After all, we'd bought it together at the same time and the same store. Seeing it on someone else had been like having a glass of ice-cold water thrown in my face. Was that how bad I looked? Bulging thighs, bare neck and all? But Jessica continued to commend me, "You look even better than you did at the store. Nice job girl, Allison Smith-Brown would be proud." Allison Schmallison, I thought, I hated the lady anyway. But those thoughts remained behind the bewildered bars of my head and I followed Jessica to join the rest the Smith-Brown look-alikes.

That was on Friday and every Friday my family went to the mosque after school for an Islamic studies program. My mother would pick me up from my high school at 4 o'clock, pick my sister up from her junior high school, then swing by my brother's elementary school and we'd all head over to the mosque. My mother came late that afternoon. I waited for her as usual in the parking lot, but the white Mazda didn't pull in until after 4:30pm. At first I read a book, looking up every time I heard a car engine, my eyes searching for the white sedan. But at about 4:15 my eyes were on the road more than the pages of my novel, so I put the book away and allowed my eyes to dart about the lane unrestrained. When 4:25 hit, I began to get worried. I whispered a prayer to myself and tried to remember if my mother had mentioned anything about being busy after school. My mother was seldom late, and I feared that my last encounter with her would be that silly argument over my clothes. My heart beat a little faster each minute. 4:25, 4:26, 4:27, a white car turned right at the end of the street, it was a little car, a Honda Civic hatchback I think. 4:28, 4:29,

4:30, 4:31, 4:32. I could hear a vehicle approaching, I stood up to get a better view, the wheels came to a halt in front of me. My heartbeat slowly regained its normal pace as I got into the passenger's seat in the car. "Sorry I'm late," my mother said as she reversed out of the parking lot. "There was an accident on the highway" she continued.

"It's okay," I answered, "I got some reading done."

"We'd better head straight to the mosque after getting your sister and brother, there's no time to stop by at the house, we're already late as it is."

"No," I blurted out "Please can we go home just for five minutes"

"We're really late already," she answered with a puzzled look on her face "And we still have to make two stops, why is it so important for us to stop by the house? They always sell food at the mosque, if you're hungry. I'll give you some money and you can get something and eat it at the break."

"It's not about food," I whispered. I wanted to change my clothes. I couldn't imagine walking into the house of Allah looking like Allison Smith-Brown in one of her many bad movies.

"Pardon" my mother asked "I couldn't hear what you said?"

"It' not about the food" I said again, this time a little louder, "I want to change out of this awful outfit. It's uncomfortable, it looks terrible and I hate Allison Smith-Brown."

My mother smiled at the road ahead. For the first time in a long time, we agreed, and it felt good. After she picked up my brother and sister, she drove me straight home. She beamed at every traffic light we encountered, green yellow and red alike. Grinned widely at license plates, stop signs and trees, and she didn't once mention anything about being late again.

She waited in the car as I rushed up to my room. I sprinted eagerly through the upstairs hallway toward my closet, but as I passed the bathroom, something made me stop. I stepped in front of the large bathroom mirror and stared intently back at my reflection. I couldn't meet myself in the eye. I stood there for a few minutes, deep in thought. Why was it so difficult for me to face myself in the mirror, I wondered? It struck me then--that wasn't me in the mirror, or at least I wished it wasn't. I heard my mother's voice then, she was standing on the landing calling to me to hurry up.

"We don't want to be too late" she concluded as she stepped back out the front door and headed to the car. In my room, I was glad to be changing my outfit. Glad to have finally remembered that God sees me not just in the mosque, but at school and in the mall and at the movies and everywhere.

Monday was a sunny day. The morning breeze ruffled the leaves in the trees as I stepped onto the schoolyard. I could see a group of people sitting under the big oak tree. "Hey!" A voice called out from the group " We're over here." A hand was waving wildly at me and I knew that was my cue to head over there. I stepped under the shade of the tree to find my friends sitting around in what some would call a circle. "Hey, how was your weekend?" Julie asked.

"Listen, we were just discussing our plans for next weekend." Jessica's voice rang excitedly as she filled me in. "On Wednesday, Kelly Huggy is going to release her latest movie. It's called The Baby Carriage. You've got to come see it with us on Sunday. You haven't made any plans for Sunday have you?" So this was it. This is what it felt like to fit in. This is what it felt like to have a life. I could feel the adrenaline pumping through my body, I had finally succeeded on my mission for a life. Sunday. I thought for a moment, I had nothing planned for Sunday. "Sunday it is." I chimed "To the movies we go!"

The school week was flying by. Everyday at school we talked about our upcoming outing. Kelly Huggy was the hot topic of discussion for the week. We all agreed that she had a flair for picking the best roles. I quietly pointed out that she was much less annoying than Allison Smith-Brown, to which I got a mixed reaction.

"What are you going to wear to the movie?" Cecil had asked me after school as she caught up with me walking home. It was Thursday, and I still hadn't been able to bring myself to tell my mother about my weekend plans. Every time I thought about asking her, some distraction would conveniently come up, and I'd tell myself it wouldn't hurt to put it off for just one more day.

"Hmm…" I mused, "I haven't really thought about that. Should I be wearing something in particular?"

"Well, Kelly does have her own clothing line out you know, so I thought it would be cool if we all wore something she designed herself. Whatever, it doesn't really matter, but just promise me you're not going to go to a Kelly Huggy movie dressed like Allison Smith-Brown."

Don't worry, I thought to myself, I won't be dressing like Allison Smith-Brown again any time soon. I could see what was happening and I felt like I was experiencing deja-vous. I had stepped back onto the slippery slope without realizing it. I found myself remembering the girl in the mirror. Remembering the shame I felt when I saw her in me.

"Helloooooooooooo" Cecil called "Focus with me here, why are you so spacey today?"

"Oh, sorry" I said.

"Don't be," Cecil ordered "because boy have I got some great news for you. Now this won't help your spacey condition, actually it will probably only make it worse, but guess what?"

"What?"

"You know Alex my boyfriend right?"

"I guess."

"Well, he's got a friend that told him he likes you," she gushed. "Do you remember Josh from science class, he sits behind that really annoying girl, Yana?"

"Josh?" I replied meagerly.

"Yeah Josh, from science class. You know the one with the funky hair that changes, like, every week? Well, anyway, he wants to come with us to the movies on Sunday. And he wants to sit beside you."

"Oh" I said.

The slippery slope had just become a lot more slippery. What had I become, I thought to myself. What kind of girl did Cecil think I was? Had I strayed so far that I was giving off the impression that I didn't mind getting chummy with boys? Did I have a big sign on my forehead that read: whitewashed? Had I become so desensitized that I could no longer differentiate between right and wrong, no longer do what was right and avoid what was wrong? I thought back to Wednesday. Thought back to the conversation Jessica and Erin had had, the coarse words they had used. Why hadn't I said anything to them? Why hadn't I asked them to stop swearing like that? I could have at least gotten up and left myself. But instead I had just sat there, allowing their words to sting me, tolerating their offensive language, excusing the assault on my ears.

Cecil's confession had been a wake up call for me. It had made me realize that the business of having a life wasn't for me. No. I preferred to have a hereafter. So I decided to step off the slippery slope before I came crashing down at the bottom. Just when I had finally started to fit in, I stepped back and pulled myself out.

I called Jessica on Saturday to tell her I wouldn't be coming to the movie.

"Why not?" she had asked, "What's up?"

"Nothing," I answered, "I've got a few other things I've got to do. But maybe we could meet up sometime after school and work on that math assignment together."

There was a long silence on the other end. Long and awkward. If ever I wondered what shock sounded like, I now knew. For a moment I thought Jessica had hung up on me. I waited for the dial tone to ring in my ear, but it never came. Instead I heard her take a slow deep breath followed closely by a single mutter: "Oh" she said flatly. She paused for a moment longer, as if to give her words a dramatic effect, "Well, then, I guess I'll see you on Monday." The phone clicked and I was left thinking about what Monday would have in store for me.

I thought about my decision a lot that weekend, but I never came to the point of regretting it. I remembered Jessica's withdrawn sigh as it drifted across miles of airwaves, making it's way over from her house to mine. I recalled her eager voice as she announced the upcoming movie title. Her abrupt and formal goodbye often diffused its way into my memory. I retained all of it. For after we hung up, the conversation wasn't over. Rather, it continued to exist within me. And I continued to nurture it, encouraging its inner survival because it represented strength and not regret. Regret was what I felt when I did things I knew were wrong just to please my classmates. Regret was what struck my spirit when I dressed in a way that made me cringe every time I saw myself in the mirror. Regret was what lurked inside of me when I was in constant conflict with the one person on this Earth that loved me even more than I loved myself, my mother. Refusing Jessica's request was a symbol of success to me. Something to celebrate, not to regret. If I had to do it all over again, I would tell her no just the same. And of course, I would have to do it all over again. After the hype about "The Baby Carriage" died down, "The Merchant of Moscow" would be released, followed quickly by "Jerry and Me". Then Allison Smith-Brown and Kelly Huggy would team-up for "Doomsday Daycare" and Gusto Maverick's half-brother, Lucky Maverick Jr., would make his big debut in a movie ironically entitled "Unlucky Ways". The end of the movie machine was nowhere in sight, and for a very good reason: there is no end. Movies are a big business that make big money. And as long as people continue to watch, Allison Smith-Brown and the like will continue to give mediocre performances. They hardly care about the messages they're sending, the values they're conveying and the morals they're teaching, they only care about one thing: the dough they're making. So if they weren't going to break the cycle, then I had to, and I did. The phone call was a step in the right direction, but it definitely wasn't the last step. Judging by Jessica's response to my response to her invitation, she wasn't very happy about being rejected. But the truth is I wasn't rejecting her, but rejecting her actions. It wasn't Jessica I was trying to avoid, but the never-ending cycle of movies. I wanted to stop the procession of movies from marching into my life and parading their filth around for me to see. I don't believe I was put on this Earth to hold the record for champion movie watcher of the year. For me, life has a greater purpose than that. The reason for my existence is in no way tied into the latest new release, or the hottest new "star". Stars are supposed to guide you with their vibrant light, but these "stars" are in need of some guidance of their own.

There was a time when I looked up to these people, looked longingly upon their posh mansions and consumed every bit of information available about their existence. I could tell you who Allison Smith-Brown hung out with on her lazy Sunday afternoons, or precisely how Gusto and Lucky Jr. were related. But at the last Friday session at the mosque, my teacher had said something that made me question that. She spoke of the absolute horrors of the Day of Judgment. On that day, she said, everyone will desert each other. Husbands will desert their wives, friends will leave one another high and dry, and even mothers will abandon their children. It's sad and very scary, but also very true. No one will have time for anyone else, for people will be too overcome with their own problems. As she uttered these unsettling words, I began to grow very alarmed. I felt chilly suddenly and my eyes fell to the goose bumps on my arms. But just then she paused; she looked at us sideways and began to speak more passionately then before. "There is one person though," she said "who will care for you on that ghastly day." She continued, "There is one person who you can turn to and plead your case. One person who will take the time to listen and help you escape the horrors of that day. One great person." She paused again, and turned her body sideways as if to conceal her face from us. It looked as if she might have been fighting back some tears. I thought of this person who would offer me some aid on a day when mothers would forget their own children's names. Who was this great person that moved my teacher to tears just at the very thought of him? Who would offer me hope in a day of desperation? I heard a girl beside me whisper a majestic name, the soft murmur of her voice struck my ears powerfully.

"It's the Messenger Mohamed," she said. The teacher turned to face us now, her eyes watering, she gazed at us tenderly, no longer trying to hide her tears. It wasn't Jessica who would stand by me on that dreadful day. It wasn't Allison Smith-Brown or Gusto Maverick. It wasn't even my mother, father, sister or brother. It was a man that had never even met me, but loved me and worried about me nevertheless. It was the greatest man to ever walk this Earth. And I knew less about him than I knew about some stupid actress. I could recite Kelly Huggy's famous friend's names but I couldn't even tell you the names of the companions of the Prophet. The Prophet who would vouch for me on the day of no assurances. The Prophet that I so often abandoned for petty things would be the only person who wouldn't abandon me in my greatest time of need.

On Monday morning, I walked across the schoolyard in search of Jessica and the rest of my friends. I found them sitting on the bench near the parking lot, and I could hear their bubbly voices dancing in the morning breeze. As I approached them, I began to make out bits and pieces of their conversation. What were they talking about I wondered to myself? My question was answered when I heard Erin gush about how funny Ms. Huggy had been as a con-nanny. Of course, The Baby Carriage, how could I have forgotten? I stepped up to the bench and stood silently for a few minutes longer.

"The best part had to be when she snagged that stuffed monkey..." Julie burst out laughing before she could finish her sentence and within seconds everyone had joined in. I smiled and looked inquiringly at Julie. "What are you guys talking about?" I asked. After regaining her breath, Julie looked over at me. "Oh, hi" she said "We were just talking about The Carriage. Why didn't you come Sunday it was great?" The Carriage, I thought to myself, so this movie had been granted an endearing nickname as well.

"Well," I began "I had some things..." But before I could finish my sentence Jessica cut in, "We know," she said "you were too busy to come." She paused and flashed me a little smirk "And as much as we'd love to explain to you what was so funny, it really was a you had to be there type of thing." The bell rang and Jessica began to collect her things. "Come on guys," she muttered "We wouldn't want to be late for first period." Somehow, I got the feeling I wasn't included in the "guys". It was just as I had suspected, Jessica felt that I had deliberately rejected her by declining her invitation to the movies and now she was going to make me pay for her pain. As I walked bleakly to my locker an old saying came to mind: with friends like those, who needs enemies?

I'll be frank with you, my walk home that day after school was miserable. Actually, it was more like a run home. It was all I could do not to burst out in tears right there in the middle of the street. Jessica had acted very distant all day. A few times, I noticed her trying to get Erin and Cecil to ignore me as well. Julie tried to comfort me saying, "Don't worry, you know Jessica, it'll pass." But as I ran home that afternoon, all I could think about was that outfit that now hung dejectedly in my closet, the sweeping shirt and the snug black pants I had bought with my friends. I can't really explain why, but I felt the overwhelming need to try that outfit on again, to see myself in it just one more time, to confirm my belief. I rummaged furiously through my closet as soon as I got home, throwing half my wardrobe on the ground before I finally found it. I pulled my school clothes off and heaved the tight black pants up past my thighs. The sweeping shirt drooped down messily, it was as if it had become even more sweeping since our last encounter. I stepped in front of the mirror and stared at the girl I saw. The girl in the mirror didn't respect herself, respect her body. The girl in the mirror fervently defended what she fully knew was wrong. The girl in the mirror was more concerned with pleasing her friends and some bad actress who didn't even know she existed than with pleasing her creator. The girl in the mirror would exist no more. I stepped back from the mirror and took one final look at her. She looked back at me timidly, draping her head in shame, ready to be cast off. And so we parted, and I was happy to see her go. So, as I discovered, having a life turned out to be more of a hassle than a hooray, more of a bother than a blessing, more of a nuisance than a nice time. If having a life meant living as a slave and servant to my fellow humans (including Allison Smith-Brown, Gusto Maverick and Kelly Huggy), then I guess it's just not for me, because I'd rather live as a slave and servant to God.

Behold

When you look at me, what do you see?
Do you see oppression and misery?
Do you see a cage enclosing me?
What do you see when you look at me?
I'm curious to know if it's sorrow or glee?
Is it freedom or slavery?
Do you see in me the weakness of a fallen tree?
A nation plagued by calamity?
If you'll look just a little bit closer you'll see
A life of fulfillment and reason to be
A content that escapes even the most wealthy
Resonates inside of me
My roots are strong like my decree
In my hands I hold life's answer key
The twisted road can no longer be
In my presence despair will flee
So take a step back and look once more
At this beautiful faith that feeds the core
Throw away the lies and propaganda
This faith only follows God's agenda
With an open heart and an open mind
Behold this marvel, the only one of its kind

Hijab: Oppression or Liberation?

"**L**OOK at these poor, oppressed women who are forced to hide behind all those clothes, so their fathers and husbands can control them. Why can't they be liberated, like me, and wear mini-skirts and swimsuits in public?"

That is what I used to think when I would see women wearing hijab. That was before I converted to Islam.

I was born and raised in various suburbs throughout the Midwestern U.S. and from as early as I can remember, I was arguing with my sexist uncles about how women were equal to men, and saying that whatever men can do, women can do better. I had friends who had bumper stickers that said things like, "A woman without a man is like a fish without a bicycle," (meaning that women don't need men) and "Behind every strong woman is herself," which was a spin-off from the saying, which feminists saw as degrading, that "Behind every strong man is a woman." My mother, who was a housewife, encouraged me to take my education seriously, which I did, because with it, I could become anything I wanted to be. My father encouraged me to take sports and physical activity seriously, which I also did. In school we learned about the suffragettes who fought for women's right to vote in the early 1900s. And through the various teen magazines, musical artists, folk singers and pop stars, I first learned about the feminist movement that took place in North America during the 1960s and 70s. Thanks to that movement and its fearless leaders, I was told, North American women had struggled, fought for, and won rights and respect they had never known before. Women were no longer forced to stay home and raise the kids, wasting their intelligence and talents on cooking and cleaning. They were pursuing their education, entering all areas of the workforce, earning as much money as men, and most importantly, being respected regardless of what they looked like or how they dressed. These feminists taught us that our looks are not what is important, therefore we can dress however we want and men should respect us nonetheless. As a result, women who wore hijab were seen as oppressed for many reasons. For example, a feminist might say that a hijabi is oppressed because the men around her are too protective of her to let her show her beauty in public. Or she might say that men and women are equal and should be held to equal standards. Therefore, if men do not have to cover their hair, then women should not have to either.

Feminists say: "I want to be respected for who I am and what I think, not for what I look like or what I am wearing. And it is up to men to change the way they look at me, no matter how I dress. It is not up to me to change my ways just because boys are stupid and cannot control themselves. Parents in our society need to raise their boys, and teach them in school, in a way that promotes an attitude that girls are not sex objects, and you should not gawk at them, whistle at them, or make sexual comments to them, or about them, to your buddies. If parents would simply teach this to their boys, then girls would not have to wear hijab. I should not have to wear hijab. I should not have to go through the inconvenience of covering my head when it is hot outside, while the boys around me are wearing shorts and T-shirts. If the boys are the ones with the problem, let the boys change. Why punish the girls for the boys' misbehaviour? Make the boys change their behaviour so I can dress the way I want to.

This is part of what feminists say about how relations should be between men and women in our society, and at a certain time in my life, I fully and wholeheartedly believed it and agreed with it.

Once I became Muslim, however, I started reading about how "men and women are equal but inherently different." At first, I thought this was just another cover for oppressing women. So I read anything I could find regarding the inherent differences between men and women. But reading about it was not enough. So I decided to start observing. I wanted to really examine the society around me and see how people behave. I did not want to read any more feminist theories against hijab or hear anymore Muslim scholars shouting at me that I have to wear hijab for my protection and that if I do not wear it, I will be causing fitnah (damage) to society. I wanted to find out for myself the real effects of hijab vs. no hijab in real life – in my life.

When I started the process of observing the society around me, I already knew that hijab is a mandatory part of the religion and that I would have to wear it someday, but I did not really understand why. I needed to understand why before starting to wear it. And I wanted to understand why. I did not want to be a hypocrite and wear it just because some sheikh on an Islamic website told me I have to. If I were to do that, I would not be able to answer questions about why I wear it. Then people would look at me as if I were a poor, ignorant, oppressed girl and they would lose respect for me, which I think would defeat the purpose of wearing hijab. Because isn't hijab supposed to be a symbol that means you want to be respected? I think it is. Therefore, I would have to understand why I am wearing it so I could explain it to others, be convinced that I want to wear it, so that others could see that I am not brainwashed and oppressed, and not be ashamed of wearing it so people could see that pleasing Allah is more important to me than pleasing others or meeting society's standards.

At the same time, I did not want to be a hypocrite by saying I am Muslim while being afraid to act and dress like a Muslim. If I were to do that, I would be no different from non-Muslims. The only difference would be that I cover myself five times a day to pray.

Contradictions

As I was observing people around me in my everyday life, I started to notice many contradictions that I had been trained never to notice before. The contradictions were between what I had learned from feminists about the way men and women should behave with each other, and what my observations were telling me about how men and women actually behave with each other.

Contradiction number one

First of all, I started looking at what girls and guys wear, and at what kind of clothes are sold for both of them in the stores. In theory, if we Westerners see men and women equally, then their clothes should be relatively equal, right? Similar styles for similar humans, right? Wrong.

When I started paying attention, I realized that guys' clothing overall is loose, long and large while girls' clothing is generally tight, short and small. Too small. The smaller the better. And it does not matter which clique you belong to, the trend is the same. Among the jocks, although the guys may sometimes wear tight T-shirts to show off their muscles, you can bet they never wear tight pants or tight shorts, while girls work out in spandex running shorts and sports bras, showing off everything they have (or don't have) for all the world to see.

The punks and skaters are the same: the guys wear long, baggy pants or shorts that go below their knees and long, loose T-shirts, while the girls wear hip-huggers that show off their belly buttons, and small, tight shirts or spaghetti-strap tank tops.

The preps and rich kids follow this same pattern. The only difference is that the guys' loose, Polo shirts and khakis and the girls' short skirts and tight blouses are twice as expensive as everyone else's.

When I walk around downtown during a summer day, I can see that the trend is exactly the same among adults. Duh. If the fashion industry brainwashes us as youth and dictates what we wear, we are not likely to change our habits when we become adults.

Contrary to my hypothesis that girls and guys would dress similarly, I found that they actually dress very different from one another.

Guys cover everything up, and girls show as much of their skin and body shape as possible. Is this liberation for women? It sounds more like liberation for men, because now they're free to look at half-naked women whenever they want. All they have to do is go outside.

Contradiction number two

Okay, so girls and guys dress differently. Girls wear tight clothes and guys wear loose clothes. So what? We live in a society that has benefited from the feminist movement of the 60s and 70s. A society that says women can have any job they want, and they do not have to be beautiful or promiscuous to get it. Our feminist foremothers paved the way for us in this society, demanding respect from men, telling them not to judge us by our looks, but by our intelligence. Sounds pretty Islamic to me. Those foremothers must have been quite intelligent themselves. As a result of the feminist movement, the guys in our society have been taught to change the way they think about girls, right? They know they have to respect us, and if they don't, it's sexual harassment, which is a criminal offence. So in this modern, "civilized," society, women do not have to cover up anymore if they want to be respected, right? Wrong.

After observing what people wear, I started paying attention to what other people are looking at. I started watching people who were watching other people, to see their expressions, reactions, and just how long they were looking. I was amazed at what I found, and everywhere I went, I saw the same thing: on the bus, downtown, in the suburbs, in the grocery store, in the mall, at school, everywhere. This is what I saw: girls and women, teenagers and middle-aged women, ugly and pretty, thin, medium, and fat, all wearing tight clothes—some of which covered most of their bodies, some that showed a lot of skin—and the girls and women generally were not looking at anyone in particular. However, when I looked around them, I saw that they were definitely being looked at. By whom? By guys: teenagers, middle-aged and even elderly men, ugly and handsome, thin, medium and fat, all wearing loose clothes, staring at the girls wearing tight clothes. Oh, be assured that they were "polite" about their staring. They did not whistle, they usually did not make comments, at least not that anyone could hear, they usually didn't grab or grope the girls (though sometimes they did), and they made sure to look away when the girls happened to look back at them. Therefore, these girls and women who were not paying attention did not realize that they were being stared at, gawked at, and fantasized about by total strangers.

The most vivid and blatant example occurred right before my very eyes on a scorching, hot and humid summer day. It happened at a time when I already wanted to wear hijab—because I knew I had to if I wanted to practice my religion correctly, follow God's orders, please God, and go to jannah—but I still did not understand why. So I was not wearing a headscarf, but I was wearing clothes that were long and loose.

I was walking down the sidewalk in a residential area of the city, near my home. Walking about 30 steps ahead of me was a girl, probably in her early 20s. She was wearing a tight, spaghetti-strap tank top and a mini skirt that went just below her rear. Her skirt was so teeny that if she had to bend over or sit, everything would have been out there for the world to see. The sidewalk was on the left side of the street, so we were walking facing the oncoming traffic. A guy, probably in his early 30s, came toward us on the street on his bike. To my amazement, he was not looking at either of us. But as soon as he passed the girl in front of me, he practically broke his neck, jerking his head around to get a look at her from behind. He kept looking backwards at her while his bike kept going forward. I just laughed to myself, thinking, "How pathetic." But the story does not end there. About 10 seconds later, he came back! He had turned around and was approaching her from behind, more slowly this time, so he could get a better look. He rode past her and made sure to stop looking before she saw him. Then he turned around again, taking a third look before going on his merry way. I could not believe it. The girl was completely oblivious to the whole thing. I am no expert on what guys are thinking about, but I am pretty sure that he was not admiring her personality, character or intellect. I often wonder whether that girl would have felt "liberated" or disgusted if she had known what that guy had done.

That incident was one of the defining moments in my understanding of why hijab is necessary. Despite our feminist foremothers' efforts to change the behaviour and attitudes of men and boys, the only thing that has changed is how blatant they are about what they do. They have learned to be more subtle, but they still look at women as sex objects who are worthy of their attention if they are beautiful and show it, and are not worthy of their attention if they are ugly or dress modestly. Personally, I do not want any guy, whether he is good-looking or ugly, young or old, to look at me like that with fantasies running through his head. Nor do I want any guy ignoring me because he thinks that my body is ugly or my hair is not pretty.   If I have something to say, I want people to listen to me regardless of what I look like or how I am dressed. But in this society, and in most society of the world, women are judged by their looks, because—let's face it—they're more beautiful and attractive than men. So how can I overcome this?

Feminists say we have to change men's behaviour. But we've already proven that that's impossible, because God has created them in a certain way that no amount of training or education will ever actually overcome. So what does Islam say?

Based on all my observations, the conclusion I drew was that, if I want people to respect me for my intellect, I have to remove all other variables from the equation. And this is part of what God is telling us by requiring us to wear hijab. If I do not want someone to look at my chest, I cannot wear a shirt that clearly shows its shape or my cleavage, and expect guys not to look, because they will and they do! Instead, I should not even give them the chance to see, and wear loose shirts that cover it up. Likewise, if I do not want the guy sitting next to me in algebra class, on the one hand, to help me with the in-class assignment when I am having a good hair day and, on the other hand, to be rude to me or ignore me when I am having a bad hair day, then I should cover my hair and not let him judge me by it, because if I don't cover it, he will judge me on it, even if he does not say it to my face. And if I cover my hair and body and he treats me rudely, then I know what kind of guy he is. I know he is only interested in looking at my body, and I will be thankful that I am not showing it to him and wasting my breath on talking to him, or wasting my energy worrying or wondering about what he thinks of me, because he is not worth it. God, however, is worth every sacrifice I can make in my life, because only God can reward me for worrying about what He thinks of me and for trying to please Him, and if I do please Him, he will reward me, with jannah, insha'Allah. No approval from any guy can even compare with that.

The challenges of actually doing it

After spending about three months making these observations, and realizing that hijab really is a good and necessary thing even in this "civilized" Western country, I finally wanted to wear the hijab, and understood why. Now, I was faced with a whole new set of challenges. The following thoughts went through my head:

All the clothes I own are either too tight or too short. My long jeans are tight, my loose shirts are short-sleeved, my long-sleeved shirts are tight, my loose skirts only go down to mid-calf, and all my summer clothes are meant to be worn with sandals and no socks! I can't wear socks with this stuff. I'll look like a dork. But I don't have enough money to buy a whole new wardrobe.

Where can I buy appropriate clothes without dressing like I am from another country? I am from North America. I would look silly wearing a Pakistani outfit or an Egyptian jilbab. How can I wear hijab, still be myself, and still be fashionable?

I don't have any headscarves or enough to match all my outfits.

I can't figure out how to wear this thing without it falling off my head or choking me! How do all those sisters do it? I wish my mother or aunt or sister were Muslim so they could teach me. I don't have anyone to teach me. Besides, no matter how I wear it, it just does not look good on me.

I have been around all these people—my classmates, teachers, friends, and teammates—and they have all seen me without hijab. If I start wearing it, they are going to think I am silly, they are not going to understand why I am wearing it now if I did not wear it before, and they are going to ask questions that I will not know how to answer or will not want to answer.

Then there is my family, who are not Muslim. What are they going to say? Are they going to ridicule me? Be ashamed to be seen with me in public? Make degrading comments under their breath or behind my back about me?

Even though I wanted to start wearing hijab, these thoughts were nagging my mind and breaking my spirit. Sometimes, I would stand in front of the mirror crying out of frustration, because I was sick of wearing the same two outfits that I owned that were the right specifications, or because I couldn't figure out a good way to wear the headscarf that was still practical and comfortable.

However, I tried to be as patient as possible, and do the best I could with what I had. I started out wearing long pants and shirts, even though sometimes they were too tight. On my way home everyday, I would pass by a clothing store or walk through the mall, just to look, and sometimes I would find one shirt, or one pair of pants, or one skirt that was on sale and that fit the way I wanted it to. I learned to go with neutral colours at first, so I could easily mix and match the few articles of clothing I owned. Finding clothes that are appropriate for hijabis is not easy in most women's clothing stores, but sometimes God makes you go into a store or turn your head toward just the perfect thing, and you say alhamdulillah. Buying clothes gradually like this allowed me to avoid the problem of being pressured into dressing like I'm from another country and allowed me to not to lose my sense of style or feel like I was dressing like an old lady. I just kept praying that God understand my situation, and forgive me for not being perfect, accept my efforts as I kept trying to improve, and make it easier for me to find modest clothes.

As for my self-pity about not having a Muslim mother to teach me how to wear hijab, I realized that there are a lot of sisters whose mothers do not wear hijab, even though they are Muslim. Those sisters had to figure it out on their own, just like me. The other thing I realized was that there were other people I could ask for help. Before I started wearing hijab, and even after I started wearing it, every time I would visit a sister or group of sisters in their home, I would ask them to take me in front of a mirror and show me how they do it. I quickly learned that there are tons of different styles of headscarves and even more ways to wear them, and each sister has her own little trick that works for her. Even now that I wear hijab, I still ask sisters to show me how they put theirs on, and what kind of fabrics work for their hair. When I go home and try out these new ideas, sometimes it works and sometimes it doesn't. But with their help, I have finally figured out a few different ways that work well for me. In addition, as with my wardrobe, I started off with neutral colours so I only needed two or three hijabs that I could match with every outfit. And once I found some comfortable, practical ways of wearing it, I did not feel self-conscious about how I looked anymore. I started feeling like I actually look good in hijab.

Starting to wear hijab around people who have known you your whole life, or for a long time, can be a scary thing to think about. I was most afraid of the questions they would ask me. To deal with this fear, I, once again, did not rely on myself, but on the guidance of God and on the experience and wisdom of other sisters. In addition to asking sisters to show me how to wear hijab, I also asked many of them why they wear it. I asked them all the typical questions: "Why do you wear it? Isn't it uncomfortable? Isn't it hot in the summer? Why don't men have to cover their hair? Can you play sports? Can you go swimming?" and so on.

I found the best answers to these questions not from books written by some sheikh somewhere about why we have to wear hijab, but from local sisters who understood what it was like to wear hijab in North America, and what it meant for us here. Many of their answers were very practical. One told me that she no longer wanted the boys bothering her at school. Another told me that she was sick of changing her clothes when it was time to pray salah, and wanted always to be wearing clothes that she could pray in. Yet another told me that it didn't matter to her whether it prevented guys from looking at her, or whether guys had problems controlling themselves. The only thing she cared about was pleasing God and following His orders because she so desperately wants to go to jannah.

To the questions about it being uncomfortable, I heard many sisters say, "You get used to it," which I have since found to be true. I heard others say, "Often, I don't even notice it anymore, and forget to take it off when I get home," and "I sometimes even feel uncomfortable without it." I think the best answer to the question of "Isn't it hot in the summer?" was "Yes, but it's a lot hotter in hell, and you can't turn on the air conditioning in hell." Since wearing hijab, I have experienced all of these feelings and situations. Interestingly enough, I used to have nightmares about going to school naked or wearing my pyjamas. Now I have nightmares about going to school without my hijab! That is how much I love to wear it and hate not to wear it!

In short, I have found that educating yourself and equipping yourself with the tools to face the opposition and the questions that you will be asked, together with the right intention and prayer that God make it easy for you and reward you for you efforts, are the best ways to prepare. And when answering questions, being straightforward and honest is the best way to earn people's respect. Even if they do not fully understand or agree with you, at the very least they will respect you.

Finally, there is the issue of dealing with my non-Muslim family. They ask the same questions that strangers do, but are more persistent about it. Sometimes they are degrading and insulting, and even more closed-minded than strangers, perhaps because they are closer to me and love me more than strangers, and want to be sure that I am doing what is best for me. Unfortunately, I do not have a good answer for how to deal with this issue yet. It is something that I am still working on and praying to God to help me with.

I started out by answering my family's questions, until I realized that some of them were not asking the questions to truly try to understand, but to use my answers against me as proof that I am wrong and they are right. Therefore, I stopped trying to convince them of my beliefs. Remember, only God can guide those whom he wants to, and if they refuse to understand, they will not be guided. Instead, I patiently let them express their opinions, even when they are angry and insulting to me, because I know it is not them talking. It is their anger and Shaytan talking through them.

I respect what they have to say, and I don't talk back or make insulting comments in return, because that only makes the situation worse and gives them a bad representation of Muslims. Most importantly, I do not compromise on what is obligatory. I know that I have to wear hijab, no matter what my family says. When they give me a hard time about it, I have to be persistent, strong, and patient, and God will reward me for the difficulty they are putting me through. I also remember that God could be putting me through much greater and more difficult tests, such as hunger or poverty, and I have to be thankful for this test, and make every effort I can to pass it and please God. I can assure you that nothing is more liberating, both in this life and in the hereafter insha'Allah, than pleasing God.

The Clash with Mr. Kensing

P. KENSING. She read the name on her schedule aloud to herself as she wandered through the busy halls in search of room 206. Her eyes leapt from door to door, scanning the rusty silver numbers. She walked slowly in small uncertain steps, trying to avoid collisions with the various objects in her path—school bags, outstretched legs, an overhead projector on a cart, but most of all other lost and wandering students like herself. It was Selma Ayman's first day of high school and she'd started it off by accidentally colliding with another frosh back near the main entrance. They had both been walking with their heads down studying their schedules. Selma's new and unmarked books had tumbled out of her arms and lay sprawled out on the tile floor. Now she was searching frantically for her next class. 208, 209, 210A, 210B. She'd missed it. She turned around and walked back up the hall she had just come down, maneuvering her way through the ever-growing swarm of students. She checked her watch—12:27.

She'd begun her classroom hunt bright and early. She'd eaten her lunch in a hurry so that she could find her next class before the bell rang and not be late on the first day of high school. It was something she'd promised herself she'd never do, for after two months of summer vacation she'd surely gotten enough rest to be able to make it to class on time. But she hadn't counted on this—crowded hallways, that seemed to bear a striking similarity to an obstacle course, and worse yet, missing room numbers. Room 206 was supposed to come before room 208 and 209, but in this hallway the laws of numerical order apparently didn't apply. The bell rang. Panic struck her and her heart thumped as she looked up to see a massive herd of students marching toward her. She gripped her books tightly and flattened herself against a locker in hopes of avoiding any bodily harm. When the flock had past, followed shortly thereafter by a few stragglers, she took a deep breath and braced herself. 'Forth to 206' she thought—'I will find this classroom if it's the last thing I do.' She walked up and down the hall a few times searching madly for the two missing classrooms, 206 and 207. How was this possible? How could a school just forget that after 205 comes 206 and before 208 comes 207? How could they just leave out two perfectly good and worthy numbers? Just then she saw something she'd missed the first 3 times she'd come up and down the now empty hallway. Just beyond the corner behind the big hall doors she caught a glimpse of a little hallway—and two classroom doors. So this is where two fine numbers had been cast off to. She stepped up to the second door on her right. The silver numbers hung loosely on their nails, they were rustier than the others. 206. She turned the knob and quietly slipped into the room. As she hesitantly walked to an empty desk, she heard a sarcastic voice fill the room.

"How wonderful," the voice boomed "someone who doesn't mind being used as an example of exactly what not to do in high school." The voice paused for a moment and then concluded with a bang: "You're late!" it snapped.

She stopped in her tracks, realizing that the voice was addressing her, she timidly turned around to face the teacher. She could hardly believe that such a big and burly voice came from such a small man. He was a skinny guy, who looked like he could have been a student at the school himself not long ago. Looked like he could have been a senior standing behind her in the cafeteria line or sitting at the activities table trying to recruit participants for the great grad trip. Even his outfit had student written all over it. His red and blue striped polo rugby shirt hung loosely out of his worn denim jeans. She noticed too that he wore Fubu sneakers. They were black with white rims, laced only half way up. She looked up to meet his gaze now, fidgeting nervously with her hijab, he was staring at her inquisitively as if waiting for a response.

"I…I'm sorry sir, I got a little lost. I….uh…couldn't….um…seem to find this hallway here."

She could here a few chuckles going around the room and one boy at the back was trying to get the class to join him in chanting "de-ten-tion" in three swift syllables.

The teacher flashed a dirty look to the class and raised his hand in silence. "This is a school, not a maze" he retorted back. "I'm not familiar with which fine scholastic establishments you all came from, but here at Charlotte Ellis Secondary School everyone is expected to be on time." He turned his attention to the entire class for this last bit, and then he looked back at her still standing rigidly between two rows of desks. "Have a seat!" he barked, gesturing with his hands to one lone empty desk at the back of the classroom. "And do make certain you spend some additional time getting well acquainted with Charlotte's web after school today so that this sort of conduct doesn't become a habit."

Of course this was just the way Selma dreamt of starting high school, not five minutes into class and the teacher already seemed to hate her. With her head lowered, she made her way to the back of the classroom and settled silently into the last empty desk.

As the days passed and her first year of high school got well underway, she became painfully aware of the reason behind Mr. Kensing's harsh welcoming words.

If she thought she had seen the worst of Mr. Kensing, she was wrong. As the year began to take shape, she began to notice a distinct pattern in her social studies class, the class Mr. Kensing taught. At first, she was happy to find that Mr. Kensing had lightened up a lot after the second week of school. He began to smile at a shocking rate and laugh at jokes other students made. Sometimes he even told jokes himself. On these days, the days of joy and laughter in room 206, the events of the first day of school seemed like a distant nightmare to her. The kind you wake up from in the wee hours of the night, sweating profusely, and thank God it was nothing more than a bad dream. When she would look at Mr. Kensing standing there at the front of the classroom, grinning widely, she could hardly believe he was the same small man who had greeted her so unkindly on that first day. But just as that horrible day began to fade into a vague memory, Mr. Kensing began to revive it and bring his legacy back to life.

"Social studies ladies and gentlemen," Mr. Kensing began, "is the systematic study of the development, structure, interaction and collective behaviour of organized groups of human beings. It is the science of society, social institutions and social relationships."

It was the third period of the third week of school and the entire social studies class looked utterly baffled by the mumbo-jumbo definition they had just heard. Mr. Kensing surveyed his student's faces for a minute and then broke out into laughter.

"Judging by your clueless faces" he said between fits of intense chuckles "you didn't like that definition of social studies too much. Well, I'll have you know that that very definition I just told you comes from a prize winning textbook written by a top professor at Harvard University. But then again, most of you probably think Harvard is a fast food chain where you can super-size your fries for only 50 cents."

His laughter subsided as he seemed to come to the sudden realization that he had been thinking aloud. The class continued to stare at him but now with looks of wild confusion plastered on their faces. Mr. Kensing took a deep breath and went on.

"In this class we'll be focusing on how the family, the individual and the society vary from culture to culture. Not everyone lives like us North Americans you know and it's important to learn the ways of other cultures so that if and when you interact with them you know what to do."

There was something about the way he said that last sentence that made Selma uncomfortable. He seemed to be speaking of 4 headed creatures on Mars, not normal humans that lived in different countries. But it was entirely possible that Selma misheard him. After all, ever since she came in late on that first day of school she'd been banished to the only available desk located at the very back of the classroom. In the back, she quickly discovered that she was surrounded by impending troublemakers. She would strain her ears to hear Mr. Kensing's lessons, but his voice had to compete with Travis Sman's wild plans for the weekend or his incessant talk of the origins of his distinguished last name. (If you must know, Travis claims his great-great-grandfather was the hero of the small town he lived in back in the early 1900's and so the town elite endowed him with the endearing nickname of Superman which was shortened to Sman for convenience over the years.) When Travis wasn't jabbering about his great-great grandfather's various bizarre but simultaneously heroic actions (like for example the time he caught a fast ball in his mouth to save a little village girl), John Whitkenbaumer was making fun of random people or trying to brainstorm different methods of escaping his inevitable detention with his troublemaker pals, Haley Henderson and Liam Krones. Once in a while, Mr. Kensing would temporarily halt his lesson and look over at the noisy mob of boys surrounding Selma's desk at the back as if he were finally going to reprimand them for their apparent inability to show any form of respect in school. But to Selma's great disappointment, he would only shake his head ever so slightly without uttering a single word of scold and continue on with his barely audible lesson. Of course, the only person who would catch the subtle shake of the head was Selma as the boys were too busy fooling around to be bothered.

A few more weeks passed as Selma worked to become adapted to the school she would call home for the next four years of her life. Overall, Selma prided herself in her relatively smooth transition from junior high school to high school. She was doing well in most of her classes, keeping up with her assignments and projects and succeeding in finding friends that she actually liked. But there was one thing about school that just didn't feel right—her social studies class. And though she didn't dread seeing Mr. Kensing everyday, she did at times get a queasy feeling in the pit of her stomach from the thought of it. She'd tried to put the embarrassing events of the first day of school behind her, but every time she'd found it in her heart to forgive Mr. Kensing for the way he'd treated her that day, he would up and do or say something else that seemed a bit offensive. But on Wednesday November 3rd, Mr. Kensing crossed the line. With Selma Ayman sitting right there in his classroom, he didn't just cross it, he stomped all over it until it was as if the line had never even existed.

The class had began as usual with Mr. Kensing first exchanging a few jokes, not entirely fit for school, with the popular group that sat in the middle of the classroom. After he'd attempted to impress them, he would talk briefly about the strange quirks of various other teachers in the school (for example Mr. Quinn, the music teacher, who wouldn't answer his office phone until he first tapped his nose). This would go on for about 5 minutes at which point Mr. Kensing would turn and yell at all the students who were talking to be quiet and shortly after he would begin his lesson. This was the routine that took place every weekday at 12:30 in room 206, it wasn't a very good routine, but it was a routine nonetheless. Over the months, Selma had gotten used to figuring out what Mr. Kensing was saying through the continuous chatter of Travis and his posse. As a matter of fact, she credits the boys for helping her become skilled at reading the teacher's lips. She'd thought of approaching Mr. Kensing about a month back to see if there was any way she could change her seat so she could actually hear something other than Liam and Haley's impersonations of Mr. Quinn. But the day she had worked up the courage to go speak to him after class, something had happened that made her change her mind. As she approached Mr. Kensing in the hall, she overheard a snippet of his conversation with Mr. Guale, the math teacher. He seemed to be discussing a student in his second period history class.

"...and then she expects me to change things around for her. Some students just don't understand that the class is set up a certain way for a reason. Teenagers think they know everything."

Selma had taken that as a sign. So she'd resorted to straining her ears and reading his lips instead, closely examining every motion and activity of his mouth until a particular word emerged. Today the boys were especially rowdy because Mr. Quinn had caught a nasty cold which left his vocal cords in an awkward condition. Mr. Kensing stood by his desk, organizing a stack of papers. He evened out the sheets with his hands and looked up, ready to start his lesson for the day.

"Okay class, today we'll be looking at the wedding traditions of different cultures." He spoke for a while about Japanese and Korean wedding customs, and then he went on to talk about the process of marriage in different parts of Africa.

"Now in Africa, there is a large majority of Moslems, and Moslems believe in arranged marriages," he said, putting some extra emphasis on the word arranged "In an arranged marriage, the bride and groom meet each other for the first time on their wedding day. If you ask me, it's a foolproof plan for a miserable marriage. But then again, I'm here to teach not to judge." If Mr. Kensing really believed he wasn't there to judge, then why had he just passed harsh judgment on the issue in front of 29 impressionable young minds?

Selma sat silently stunned. Had she heard him right? Maybe Haley Henderson's attempt to imitate Mr. Quinn had affected her hearing. But as much as she would have loved to blame this one on Haley's lame impersonation, the sad truth lingered in the back of her mind: Mr. Kensing was knowingly or unknowingly teaching the class false information about Islam. And it made Selma furious. But sitting there tucked away at the back of the classroom with her violet hijab wrapped carefully around her head, she couldn't bring herself to say anything. She tried to raise her hand in defiance, lift it high up into the air and put an end to the lies. But instead she found herself sitting motionless in her seat, the loud pounding of her heart drowning out the shrill voice of Travis Sman.

Selma spent the rest of that day upset. Upset that in a place of knowledge such ignorance would still exist. Upset that Mr. Kensing would dare spread such falsehood about Islam with a visibly Muslim girl sitting right there in his classroom. But mostly, upset that she didn't have the guts to do anything about it. She had just sat there and listened to the lies as if she didn't know any better.

Selma didn't sleep too well that night. The small bouts of sleep she did eventually get were filled with dreams too absurd to remember. She woke up with this uneasy feeling, as if she hadn't spent the last 7 hours tossing and turning in bed but rather under great oppression. She couldn't stop thinking about the previous day's social studies class. It was as if her mind was tied to a short and sturdy leash, whenever her thoughts wandered slightly off to thinking about little things like what she was going to pack for lunch that day, it was abruptly yanked back to remembering Mr. Kensing's awful lesson. The worst part was that the lesson was not over, it was an entire study unit that would take about a month to complete according to her course schedule.

That day in social studies Mr. Kensing didn't do much talking. Instead he distributed a handout to the class that would do his dirty work for him while he marked some assignments at his desk, where the traditional teacher's apple was replaced by his daily can of Coca Cola. Selma read and reread the paper in front of her in disbelief. Where did he get this stuff, she wondered? It was as if Mr. Kensing had access to some library that was full of false information about Islam. After marriage, Muslim women are expected to stay home and most do not complete their education.

The task of choosing his daughter's husband is given to the Father in Islam.

Selma couldn't believe her eyes. She skimmed the rest of the article and found it to be littered with similarly false statements. She couldn't make any sense of it, and for good reason: it didn't make any sense. She turned her paper upside down and pretended to look busy taking notes, but really she was busy thinking about this whole affair. She was a religious Muslim and came from a religious family yet her mother had a Master's degree and a career. Her older sister, who had just gotten married this past summer had met and gotten to know her husband well long before their wedding day. And her father, a very gentle and in no way oppressive man, hadn't made the final decision on who her sister would marry, her sister had. Why then was this article so radically different from the truth? With her heart thumping louder than a basketball's noisy bounce, Selma decided she would put an end to this nonsense right then and there. Her palms began to sweat and she could feel her fingers trembling as she raised her right arm into the air. Travis Sman turned from the conversation he was having with Liam Krones to watch Selma's hand rise up. He looked skeptically over at her and said: "What are you doing? You're going to draw Kensy's attention over here!"

"That would be the point" Selma retorted back. Her fury with the article had given her a burst of unexpected confidence. Mr. Kensing was sitting at his desk with a red pen in hand shaking his head and marking a paper. After a moment longer, he looked up from the pile of papers in front of him, letting out a deep sigh he said, "Yes Selma?"

"Um...sir...I just wanted to point out that um...this article here is not...not very a...accurate." She could barely hear her own shaky voice over the thunderous beating of her heart. Beneath the desk, her knees began to quiver.

"In what way is it inaccurate?" he questioned.

In what way is it not inaccurate, she thought to herself?

"Um...well...you see...I'm...I'm Muslim and my Mom works and is educated and also...my...my sister didn't have an arranged marriage like the article says."

Mr. Kensing smiled. "Selma."He put his pen down on the desk. "I'm not saying that your Mother is uneducated or that your sister had an arranged marriage. No. But you probably come from a very liberal household. I mean, just the very fact that you live here in North America and attend a public school tells me that you and your family are exceptions to the rule." He glanced over at the clock hanging above the door. "Okay we're running out of time so I want you to finish up the questions at the back of the article for homework, we'll take them up in class tomorrow and don't forget to go online and do that quiz I posted before Friday." The class packed up their books and shuffled out the door. In the crowded hallway Selma was deep in thought. What did he mean "liberal household", she came from an average Muslim household. It was typical, not liberal. And her family wasn't the exception to the rule, they were the rule. How could Mr. Kensing have turned this around on her? After all, she was the Muslim so shouldn't she naturally know more about Islam? Shouldn't she be the one to decide where her family fell in the wide spectrum of Muslims? She walked passed Travis Sman and John Whitkenbaumer standing in the corridor on her way to math class. Travis shot her a dirty look; he was obviously still upset that she had broken the unwritten rule of never attracting attention to the back of the classroom. "Get over it!" Selma snapped.

Selma's bus ride home that afternoon was less than pleasant, to no fault of anything but her own creative imagination. She imagined that every person that stepped onto the bus was evaluating her critically. She pictured them pitying her, judging her, gaping mockingly at her headscarf and thinking: "There she is. That poor oppressed girl." If I could read their minds right now, she thought, I'd probably wish I'd never learned to read. In her defense, she envisioned herself politely taking permission from the bus driver to use his loud speaker and making an announcement to all her fellow passengers. She would put her mouth to the intercom and declare: "I know what you're thinking and it's not true!"

As Selma stepped off the bus, she walked right passed the newspaper stand that stood outside of the bus shelter. She walked by this stand everyday, usually taking no notice of the headlines sprawled in murky black ink on the front page. But today something made her turn back. From the corner of her eye she had caught a glimpse of a large picture in the centre of the page. The young woman in the photograph wore a veil. Selma stopped to read the caption underneath the photo. *24 year old Aisha Abdullah was murdered Tuesday night by her own father because she refused to marry the young man he had chosen for her. Story continued on page B3.*

Selma searched through her wallet for 75 cents. She inserted the shiny coins into their slot and unfolded the inky paper, flipping the limber grey pages until she found the full story of Aisha. After reading the tragic tale once, she went back and counted the number of times the words "Islam" and "Muslim" appeared in the short article. Seven. Seven times did she cringe, seven sly shots did she dodge, seven printed words of deceit did she know better than to believe. Selma felt weak suddenly, she shuffled to a nearby bench and sat down before her legs gave way beneath her. What's the matter with this world, she thought. Was it a new trend to link the beautiful religion of Islam to every possible atrocity? The article had stated: *Ali Abdullah, the victim's father, used his religion, Islam, to justify his extreme actions.* That is ridiculous, she thought. So ridiculous because of the very fact that the religion of Islam was sent to put an end to unjustified killings like these. She folded the newspaper in half and tucked it under her left arm in hopes of concealing it from the world. She wished she could somehow empty out all the newsstands from the lies they were selling. It wouldn't be enough to make that announcement using the intercom on the bus, she'd need a very large megaphone if she wanted to make any sort of difference. Selma heaved herself off the bench, she felt heavy, like the burdens of the entire world were resting on her shoulders. Lugging her school bag, she walked home wondering what people would think of her when they laid eyes on her hijab. Would they think she was oppressed like the media told them? Would they think she was uneducated like they were taught in school? Selma found it quite ironic that she was in fact a top student in her school and that out of all her non-Muslim friends father's, hers was probably the calmest. Her father never came home drunk at one in the morning like Alicia's or threatened to kick her out of the house at 18 like Diana's.

When Selma finally got home that day, she was totally drained. She left her social studies homework until the very end because she couldn't bear the thought of having to read that nonsense again. She stared blankly at her chemistry notes. But instead of H_2O, she saw Aisha's somber face sprawled across the front page. In place of $NaCl$ and $K+$, she saw Ali Abdullah being handcuffed and dragged to court. The next few weeks of school seemed to crawl by at an exceedingly slow rate. The queasy feeling that Selma used to occasionally get before her social studies class was now a regular visitor. She spent most of her lunch hours dreading what was to follow—her social studies class, or as she had secretly begun to refer to it, her Islam-bashing class. Selma seemed unable to focus lately. She constantly felt tired and lacking in energy. She had actually begun to appreciate Travis and John's steady ranting. Liam and Haley also did their part in drowning out the nonsense Mr. Kensing was teaching at the front of the classroom. It hadn't always been like this. Selma had tried time and again to politely correct Mr. Kensing's inaccurate lessons on Islam. She'd defied Travis Sman's back-of-the-classroom regulations so many times that he had given up hope in her and had eventually stopped eyeing her rudely. But Mr. Kensing hadn't responded to Selma's comments and feedback very well. He was the teacher, and as such he believed he should do all the teaching, even if that meant sacrificing its quality. Every time Selma tried to contradict Mr. Kensing's teachings, he would come up with some excuse in his defense, reminding her that her, her family and her friends were all liberal exceptions to the rule. That's when Selma had begun to get frustrated and lose hope, allowing herself to retreat into the shadow of the back of the classroom. She felt she wasn't learning much from his class. But if there was one thing Mr. Kensing had taught Selma it was that, contrary to what she believed as a child, not all teachers are necessarily fit to be role models.

On November 16th Mr. Kensing announced to the class that their unit was almost over.

"It's your turn now." He explained, "Pick a topic related to what we've just been studying, get it approved by me and then follow the guidelines in this handout and Voila—you have your research project." He walked around the classroom, handing out a single sheet of paper to every student. "You'll be handing in a written report and doing an oral presentation in front of the class." He continued. "You have until this Friday to choose your topic. This is your independent Study Project, your big project of the semester, so I suggest you choose your topic carefully because once you do, you're stuck with it."

Selma read over the handout carefully and found her lips involuntarily moving to form a small grin. She had gotten an idea. She would do her project on Islam. For once, she would be the one standing up there at the front of the classroom telling the class all about the real Islam instead of awkwardly struggling to correct Mr. Kensing's lies. That's right, why shouldn't she do her project on Islam? A few reasons why quickly came to mind right off the bat. For one thing, her marks would probably suffer. Knowing Mr. Kensing, he'd probably take it as a personal attack on his teaching ability. All day long, the idea tossed and turned keenly inside her head. She tried to put it aside, reminding herself that her grades would likely pay the price, but she just couldn't seem to shake it from her head.

Walking past the newsstand that day after school, Selma noticed a big headline that read: "Islamic Jihad Group Continues Vigorous

Bombing Campaign" Underneath the title was a large photograph of a bearded Arab man. Shaking her head, she continued on her way.

Sitting at home at her desk, Selma tried to think of different topics she could research. Topics she would both enjoy studying and could get a good mark in. But her mind was drawing a blank, so Selma headed down to the den to see if she could find anything on the news to trigger some ideas. She flipped around for a bit until she found an FBI show on channel 12. This looks interesting, she thought. She'd lost hope in finding anything inspiring, so she settled for something exciting instead. But her excitement was quickly replaced with fury. The theme of the show centered on finding a sleeper terrorist who was behind a huge militant scheme. The terrorist was, of course, a Muslim. Selma didn't know whether to cry from sadness or yell from anger. Her heart ached and her mind raged. Everywhere she went lies seemed to surround her. It was as if her Muslim identity had been stolen from her and thrown in a dirty pit, the grimy stains were all around her. Selma didn't know exactly what she would do or how she would do it, all she knew was that she couldn't sit passively by anymore and listen to others tell her what her religion was all about. She was the Muslim, she would do the telling from now on. She would do her research thoroughly, she would write her report eloquently, she would present her topic enthusiastically and she would come up with the best gosh darn independent study project that Mr. Kensing had ever had the pleasure of marking. If she couldn't educate the entire world about the true Islam, the least she could do was educate her 29 classmates.

On December 6th, Selma sat nervously at the back of the classroom. She could feel the butterflies in her stomach actively fluttering about as she listened to Travis Sman discuss the impact of society and culture on the origin of surnames. It was strange to hear his voice coming from the front of the classroom instead of the back. Selma was surprised to see that he looked rather nervous as he gave his oral presentation. He was nervous but also peculiarly happy that he could finally share the story of his great-great grandfather with a larger and willing audience. Though she'd heard the details of this tale so many times before, Selma almost didn't want it to end because she was up next and she was terribly anxious. But of course, it did end and before long she found herself gathering her large duffle bag of props and heading over to the front of the classroom.

Her presentation was a multimedia presentation. She had prepared an interactive jeopardy game on Islam, cued a video clip on Muslim women in Islam, brought an assortment of hijabs to put on display and interviewed a Muslim woman convert on the reasons behind her decision to embrace Islam. Selma tacked her poster up onto the bulletin board as Mr. Kensing finished grading Travis' oral presentation. She stepped back to see if it was leveled. The big bubble letters of the title jumped out at her 'Common Misconceptions about Islam', it read. She whispered Bismillah to herself and took a deep breath before looking up to meet Mr. Kensing's gaze.

"Okay Selma," Mr. Kensing said, he was sitting in her desk at the back of the classroom, "you may begin."

Selma began the presentation she had rehearsed inside out for the past week and a half. She started with a 5-minute talk about what Islam was all about, then moved on to mention the common misconceptions people had about Islam.

"And there are a lot." She pointed out. Selma than turned to her display of hijabs. She demonstrated, using a female volunteer participant from the class, how the hijab was worn and explained the reasons behind wearing it. After showing the class her video interview with Rachel, an American Muslim who had converted to Islam at the age of 18, Selma initiated a game of Islamic trivia, with prizes and all. She was amazed at the class' reaction, they were interested and interactive. Even Haley Henderson and Travis Sman were paying attention at the front and competing over who would land the double jeopardy question.

"And so," Selma concluded, "Next time you hear or read something about Islam and Muslims, ask yourself 'Does this sound reasonable?' If the answer is no, than it may very well not be true. Thank you for listening to my presentation."

Except for John Whitkenbaumer's obvious disappointment at not being chosen for the hijab demonstration, Selma felt the presentation had been a smash success. She stood at the front of the classroom for a few minutes longer, answering questions until the bell rang and the students emptied out of the classroom with their prizes of candy in hand. Selma gathered her things, placing the collection of hijabs in a bag and ejecting the videotape from the VCR. She took down her poster and rolled it up with an elastic, then with her hands full, she turned to the door.

"Ms. Ayman," she heard a voice call from the back of the classroom. The voice had paused; it was waiting for her to turn back around. Selma cocked her head a little to the right as if to check her hearing. He'd never called her that before and she wondered what had brought about this newfound respect. Experiencing a deja-vu of sorts, she turned around to look at him. Mr. Kensing was still sitting in her desk at the back of the classroom. But he got up now and approached Selma. Smiling, he handed her the marking sheet he had just finished filling out. "Excellent presentation!" he said.

So Selma learned that she didn't need a megaphone to make a difference. She didn't need a large media corporation backing her or all the newspaper stands in the world (though they definitely would help). She only needed herself, her voice, her smile, her example. She also learned that Mr. Kensing was not the enemy. Yes, he was a proud and sometimes rough man, but still not the enemy. Mr. Kensing only taught what he was taught about Islam. He taught what he had learned from the mainstream newspapers, the radio, and the 6 o'clock news. And until someone taught him differently, he could not be blamed for the inaccuracy of his ways. Until Selma Ayman taught him differently.

Bonus Bolters

W'VE all seen them. They live in our neighborhoods, shop in our malls and pray in our mosques. Sometimes, they lead us in prayer, sometimes they sit next to us at picnics, and sometimes they stand behind us in lines. You may not realize it, but you may be one yourself. They're called the Bonus Bolters and they've been around for ages.

The BB's, as they're sometimes referred to, seem to have a peculiar phobia. They appear to fear accumulating any extra good deeds. It's rather a strange concept, I know, but it has been happening time and time again in countries the world over. They coast through life on the bare minimum, accept themselves as satisfactory without bothering to try to achieve excellence. This is not to say that they are generally lacking in any way. No. As a matter of fact, many Bonus Bolters wear big hats in life. They are doctors, lawyers, teachers, engineers—they can hold pretty much any title that exists—and they work hard to achieve and keep it. But they are short sighted, only seeing so far as 20 maybe 30 years down the road, only really seeing as far as this life goes. Don't get me wrong. They are called Bonus Bolters and not Obligatory Bolters for a reason, they do what is asked of them, what is expected of them. But their tragic flaw remains.

If you ask me, if you're going to go for something, go for it all the way. Heaven is not a place you only travel half the distance for. It's worth the bumpy ride, worth the patience of a long and thorny journey. So if you get a chance to score some bonus points, do yourself a favour, don't bolt.

Consciously Aware

ON Wednesday September 12th, 2001, for the first time ever, I was consciously aware that I was different. The morning of the day before, shock had settled upon North America. My household, like millions across the nation, had been absorbed by the latest news. We gripped every piece of information, clenched new developments tightly in our frightened hands. When I got up the next day to get ready for school, my routine was the same as always, except not. As I pinned my hijab and headed for the door, I thought about what people might do, what people might say, what their eyes might say to my eyes. Or more importantly what people might not say but what they might think to themselves, which was, in a way, worse because I couldn't correct them, couldn't explain to them, couldn't try to make them understand. I stepped out the front door and I remembered, I remembered that I looked different, and for the first time in my life I felt threatened because of it. A hint of fear, a touch of blame for something I didn't do, for something I couldn't even grasp yet, for something I would never understand.

As I stepped onto the bus, the bus driver was grumpy, but he was always grumpy, was he grumpier today? Was it my imagination or were people eyeing me? Neighbours' smiles turned to frowns, people looked upset at me, ashamed of me. Was I imagining this? I may very well have been, the lady in the brown coat could be frowning because she had a bad morning, maybe she didn't have time for breakfast. But what I didn't imagine was the horrible stories I heard from my Muslim friends. "She was chased on the highway while she went to pick up her 2 kids from school. She arrived 3 hours late…she's not the kind to arrive late."

"He rolled down his car window as he approached me and began to swear. Racial slurs left his mouth and stung my ears…"

"Go home, they yelled at her as she marched to the vigil on Parliament Hill. Her Uncle had died on that day and people hassled her for attempting to mourn for him.

It was my stop, I rung the bell and got off the bus, headed toward school. Would people treat me differently? I guess I'd find out. Should I still go to the mall after school? Better not. And suddenly I was paying the price for the evil act I myself had only become aware of the morning before.

Finding My Way

CRINGING, I walk past another shop window decorated with barely clad manikins. A large poster screams out at me in big bold letters "show your collarbone" it orders. I whisper the words to myself. I'm so out of it, it seems, that I walk right into a group of girls standing by the food court. "Excuse me." I say to the mob of spaghetti strap tank tops and shorter than short shorts. My apology, however, is only met with a deep glare. One girl looks me up and down and laughs sarcastically at my wardrobe. I hear her mutter something about the North Pole and assume she is referring to my choice of pants and traditional t-shirt on this warm day.

My day continues on much the same note. My eyes rendez-vous with poster after poster of women who "dare to bare" as the ads command. Whether from the pictures in the stores or the masses in the mall, I quickly realize that there is a common theme in spring fashion this season—flesh is in, and as with every year—there is an abundance of it. This year though, yet another spin has been put on the way in which people should bare. It's called the distasteful look in which the most important thing is the amount of skin you show. A hip juts out here, a stomach bulges there, and I have a very difficult time keeping my lunch down while almost drowning in this sea of flesh.

It's hopeless, I decide, and I return home feeling that I have failed yet again. How difficult can it really be to find one long skirt without a slit? Or one long sleeved blouse that does not curve in all the wrong places? Theoretically, considering that there are hundreds of malls with thousands of stores with millions of articles of clothing in my city, it should be a piece of cake. But experience tells me that this cake is made of some very rare ingredients. This is the way my life was for about a year and a half. I was living neither here nor there, but sitting on the sidelines and watching others take shots at the ball. Every spring I was disgusted by the new fashions that came out. The new shorts of the season just a few inches shorter than those of the year before. The skirts just a little tighter and their slits just a little higher up. I watched as sleeves disappeared all together and straps became thinner and thinner. Soon after, straps were declared a terrible nuisance and were eliminated from tops all around. I watched and watched and watched, saddened by the sequential progression to nowhere, but still not strong enough to take a stand: to stand up and where the hijab. I thought about it often and would sometimes put it on in my bedroom when no one was around. I would sit with it on for hours, reading a book or doing my homework, until I would forget it was on. Then I would hear the key turning in the key-whole and I'd quickly slip it off and stuff it back into my mother's dresser, with a tang of regret. It was on these nights that I'd lay awake for hours, pledging that the next morning I would make my grand announcement. I would sit at the kitchen table, cough twice and announce that I had finally decided to wear the hijab. But the morning would come without the coughing or the announcement. I would tell myself that before I began wearing the hijab, I had to go shopping for an appropriate wardrobe. After all, the hijab is much more than a piece of cloth you wrap around your head, it's a manner of covering your entire body. So I would delay the coughing and the announcement and go shopping after school instead. But of course, upon entering the mall and seeing the ever so limited horrific fashions, I would immediately begin rotating in the vicious cycle and I'd be back at square one. Despair would overtake me and my pledge would be broken yet again. I would tell myself that it's too soon, that I'm doing it for the wrong reasons anyway, so I shouldn't do it now. And when I'd see a Muslim woman wearing hijab being portrayed negatively on television, fear would grip my heart. Fear that if I wore the hijab people would think that I was oppressed just like that fictional actress who's father and husband would take turns oppressing her. But

fear never visited me alone, it always brought a partner along—
disappointment. I was disappointed in my lack of courage to live on
the outside what I so deeply believed on the inside. Disappointed
in my failure to show the world that I had chosen the hijab on my
own and could also choose to disobey the fashion army's orders.
Disappointed in my inability to confirm that I wouldn't wear the
designated uniform that came out every season dictated to me by the
creator of capries. I would instead dress in my own style in accordance
with the guidelines of the Creator of the universe. But feeling disappointment was not enough. I could mope around for days, frustrated
and regretful about my numerous failures, but that would not change
my situation or bring me any closer to my goal of wearing the hijab.
I had to somehow get over my fears and transform my disappointment
into action that I could be proud of. Where to begin, I thought to
myself?

It's funny how, just when you think you're drowning, fate throws
you a lifeline and God sends someone to shed a little light in the
darkness. Only a few days after my last hopeless trip to the mall, something happened that really boosted my spirits. A new girl came to our
school. This was in no way anything out of the ordinary because new
people come all the time. But what was unexpected was that she was
Muslim—and she wore the hijab. Okay, so maybe that doesn't sound
so astonishing on it's own, but there's more. She wore the hijab
and was confident, intelligent, happy, well-liked, and to my delight,
very stylish! I didn't know this new girl well, she was a senior in high
school while I was still a freshman, and so we didn't have any classes
together. But I often observed her from afar, watching closely to
see how she interacted with people and how people treated her. Did
people make fun of her? Did they pity her and leave her out of their
group? Did they laugh at her for wearing the hijab? To my surprise,
the answer was almost always no. I think she began to notice that I
was watching her, she would look over at me every now and then from

across the cafeteria and smile. I imagine she thought it was strange that I was always monitoring her, after all, since I didn't wear the hijab, there was no way she could have known that I was Muslim like her. She probably thought I was some kid who'd never seen a Muslim woman wearing the hijab in her life before. And in a way I was. For through her I was learning that it was possible to demystify the stereotype of the oppressed Muslim woman just by going to school every day while wearing the hijab and setting a good example. I admired her strength. She seemed to be at such ease in her attire, people didn't even seem to notice her hijab after a while. But it wasn't like people ignored her hijab and treated her like everyone else. She was distinct yet accepted. The hijab reminded others that she had her own boundaries that were not to be crossed. It silently commanded respect.

She approached me one day. It was after school and I was crossing the football field and making my way home. I heard her jean skirt rustling behind me but dared not turn around. What could I say to her? 'I'm sorry I'll stop stalking you now.'

"You dropped a paper" I heard a soft voice behind me say. I stopped walking and turned around. "I don't know if it's important, but here it is just in case." When I looked at her she was smiling and offering out my history assignment in peace. She had kind eyes.

"Th...thank you" I stammered.

"I'm Khadija" she said "what about you?"

I have to say I was taken aback. There I was expecting her to tell me off for creeping her out by watching her all the time and instead she rescues my history project and then goes on to introduce herself to me.

"I'm Amina, and I'm Muslim too." I couldn't help it, I just blurted it out. I realized that it sounded a little awkward after I said it, but I felt relieved. I wanted her to know that I was just like her, that I believed in the same things as her even though I'd never met her before in my life. At that moment I wished more than ever that I were wearing the hijab. Wished that she and others could tell that I was Muslim just by taking one look at me. Wished that I didn't have to blurt it out awkwardly for them to know.

We saw each other a few times after that. We both became busy with school-work but would sometimes catch each other after school and walk a few blocks together until the path to our homes made us part in different directions. We often talked about the hijab when we were together. Actually, it was more like I asked her questions about the hijab and she answered. I was surprised to learn that she had faced the same difficulty as me when looking for clothes appropriate for the hijab. It was hard, she said, but you had to be persistent because every once in a while the fashion industry slips and makes something decent that we can wear. She would also get clothes sewn for her by her mother's friend and was more than happy to hook me up with her seamstress. I asked her once about how she felt when she watched the false portrayal of Muslim women on T.V. It was clear that it bothered her. If someone lied about you and your family, it would bother you too. But she told me something in regard to this that I would never forget. She said that even the light of one candle is stronger than the darkness of the entire world. She asked me to be a beam in that light.

"Don't worry about all the world's problems just yet," she'd said to me one day. "Worry about yourself for now. Make sure that you're doing what's right on your part. If everyone worries about them-selves and makes sure they do what's right, then the world will change for the better." Those were among her last words to me, for she told me on that same day that her family was moving to another city. I remember noticing when I first met her that she had kind eyes. After getting to know her I discovered that she had an even kinder heart. Long after she had gone though, her deep words lingered on in my thoughts. I had to be the change I wanted to see in the world. If I wanted the world to know that Muslim women were not oppressed, I had to show them myself. And even though I did seem to be up against the majority of the media, as Khadija had proven to me, people remember you more than they remember the fictional actress on television. You're a living, breathing human, and if you contradict what the media tells them about Islam, chances are, they'll begin to question the accuracy of what they're watching.

I realize now, that the light was probably always there, but maybe I was too overcome with darkness that I overlooked it.

An Anthropologist's Report

SHE was told broken promises were something she'd have to get used to if she traveled to this unusual land. Fake smiles and forced laughs, hugs one day and backs the next.

The language was different there too.

For it was quite common to say one thing but mean the exact opposite.

Half the time, hand gestures, body posture and uncontrollable giggles replaced verbal communication almost entirely.

It is a place where contradiction proves to be the rule and not the exception.

It has a very unique culture, they say.

Unique in that the citizens of this land make up their own rules. In fact, the only rule they all seem to adhere to, is the rule that no member should abide by any rules.

Compliance in this one rule is ensured almost entirely by fear. For the greatest fear that the citizens of this land have is rejection. To be caged in a box at the centre of the city square under a big sign reading "loner". This "caging and labeling" process guarantees that all citizens know the status of each member of this group. It also proves to result in a delightful recreational activity in which non-loner members who happen to be passing by the city square can point and snicker at the caged ones. They say there is strength in numbers, but in this society there is danger in numbers. When too many members of this particular group assemble, something strange happens. Strange but not surprising. When in groups, especially large groups, they seem to forget who they are. Seem to forget that they are indeed humans and not animals. They act in ways that are unacceptable to themselves as individuals but expected of them in groups.

Anthropologists speculate that this group fosters some very

peculiar traditions. For example, to make newcomers feel welcome, it is customary for the group elders to force the newcomers to drink a repulsive beverage in quantities that are toxic and harmful to the body and brain. Other welcoming traditions include slightly beating the newcomers, throwing them in large bodies of water, and tying them up and throwing dirty objects at them. The laws of the land are based on pleasing one another at any expense, as such, the laws are extremely volatile and can change as often as every two days. If something is declared "hip" or "cool", it is expected to be implemented by the majority of the group immediately. However, this is expected to be done in a subtle fashion in which members of the group pretend not to be too eager to adopt this new law.

It is a society that is in fact, built on solid nothing.

It's a world where the expectations change by the second.

She'd heard of many who'd entered this world and never came out on the other side.

Those who are transported to this world are often met by an inviting banner that reads: "Welcome to the world of lies, deception, awkwardness and insecurity. Welcome to the popular teenage culture."

Dreaded Days

I shouldn't have been sitting there on my couch at home that Monday morning three years ago. There was nothing physically wrong with me, no sniffle, no sprained ankle from yesterday's gym class, not even a slight itch. My problems all lay in my head. Bottled up inside, brimming and brewing like they would burst out at any moment. The couch I lay on was part of a set my mother had picked out when she first got married. The matching love seat and sofa bed sat facing me against the living room wall. They were decorated with various forms of flowers, nothing short of flower power really. Each cushion overflowed with colourful rose bushes. Lilly of the valley lay at my feet and squashed under my cheek was a white petunia. I lay there for a few minutes, thinking about the reason why I couldn't heave my little body off the couch. The two words I so dreaded to hear came to mind: high school. In my mind's eye, I saw my high school as the centre of the universe. And it being the centre of the universe and all, I couldn't easily escape it. High school dictated how I talked, how I walked, how I dressed, what I ate, who I talked to. It shaped me like play dough. It pulled my strings like a marionette. My high school, a two storey building that stood across the street from a Pizza Pizza, so fully consumed me some days, I believed nothing else mattered.

It was always the same story. The summer break was my heroic savior. It pulled me up from the deep sea I was drowning in like two strong arms. It brought me back to the surface of reality and gave me a chance to take a deep and much needed breath of fresh air. Every summer, as I would take this deep, refreshing breath far away from the pressures of high school, I would make a secret promise to not allow myself to be swept away by the pathetic teenage trends that always seemed to materialize in September. The time it gave me away from school was more precious than any other time I could get. It wasn't time in the sense of seconds, minutes and hours, it was time in the sense of life. I fear that if it weren't for those 2 months a year, I wouldn't have survived the Jungle we call high school. I wouldn't have remembered that there was so much more to life than Nike shoes and Tommy Hilfiger jeans, then looks and dances, movies and music. But there is so much more. There's family, there's work, there's love and marriage. There's your baby's first smile, first gurgle, first step. There are years and years of life's little surprises. Looking back, I know that now. Don't let four years of your existence dictate the rest of your life.

Prom

IT was the beginning of the end, the beginning of my last year of high school. Finally, I was a grad and I had the whole year to enjoy it. I walked the halls of my high school with a different feeling. My walk itself was different now. Now that it was my last year, I felt more special, more powerful, and a whole lot more like an expert. I knew all the ins and outs of Thompson High, knew every corridor and every stairway inside out, knew every short-cut and every vending machine. I had spent the last 3 years here and this was my fourth and final year. And I planned to have a really good time.

On the first day of school, I went to get my schedule for my classes and then met up with my best friend Laura for lunch and the afternoon. Laura and I had been together in elementary school and all through high school. Now we sat on the front lawn of our school, catching up on each others' summers and comparing schedules.

"Not even a single class," I said, holding up both our schedules in my hands.

"I can't believe this!" Laura pouted.

"We didn't have any classes together last year either."

"This stinks," I concluded. "No spares together. No classes together. Just lunches – great!"

"Hey Laura! Hey Fatimah!"

We looked up to see our friend Amy coming over. "Hey Amy," we both said.

"How was your summer?" I asked.

"Oh, it was okay. Pretty boring," Amy shrugged. "But I'm excited for this year, aren't you guys?"

"I'm excited for this year to end!" Laura exclaimed. "I wanna get out of this place already."

"Yeah, me too," I agreed. "But first, we get to be grads. On Traffic

Day, we won't have to follow any of these signs anymore."

"We'll be the ones holding the signs," Laura said with a grin.

"Yeah . . . this should be good," Amy nodded slowly.

"Hey – the coveralls!" Laura said. I grinned.

Amy looked at us, puzzled. "What about the coveralls?"

"We get to wear them," Laura answered.

"You know Laura," I said. "She's been waiting this whole time just to wear those coveralls. It's the only thing that kept her from dropping out!" All three of us laughed.

It was two o'clock in the afternoon, and Laura and I were on the bus going through downtown. We had decided to beat the crowd and go buy the famous blue coveralls from the store ourselves. The coveralls were the designated uniforms that grads wore for grad week – the week when grads ruled the school through spirit activities between periods and at lunch-times. Every year, we had watched others march around the halls in their blue coveralls, and now it was our turn. But instead of waiting for the grad committee to buy them from the store and then sell them to us at a higher price, we decided that we would save some money by going ahead of time and buying them ourselves from Items Second Hand Store, which was where the grad committee always bought them.

Laura and I tried on pairs and pairs of blue coveralls until we finally found the right ones. We were careful to get the exact shade of blue, that dark muted blue that grads always ruled the school in. We left the store, with our blue coveralls in our plastic bags and big smiles on our faces. We were all set – now we just had to wait for grad committee to announce Grad Week.

We had no idea just how long we would have to wait for that announcement. The first week of school went by, and nothing. Then the second and then the third. Still nothing. Then the fourth week.

The first month of school had passed with no Grad Week. On the fifth week of school, grad committee announced that next week was Grad Week. 'Finally,' I thought.

Friday after school was time for everyone to come purchase their coveralls and decorate them. I met Laura at her locker and we headed down the hall to help carry the paint and brushes out to the back field. As we headed out the school's back doors, our hands barely hanging on to the six buckets of paint, we squinted in the sun.

"Laura . . ." I said slowly, looking at the coveralls on the field.

"Keep walking Fatimah," she urged. "This paint is heavy."

"Then put it down," I said, putting down the three buckets that I was holding.

"What's wrong with you?" Laura put the buckets down and looked at me.

"They're white," I said, pointing to the coveralls on the field.

Laura looked at the field and saw one white coverall after the other after the other. None of them were blue. We had the only two blue coveralls in the whole school. This was ridiculous.

Disappointed as we were, we started feeling better little by little as we decorated our coveralls, painting inside jokes and special nicknames that we had earned throughout the last three years. With our coveralls painted and ready, we sat around and let the sun dry them. It was a beautiful afternoon, I was sitting there with Laura and my other friends and we were chatting, chatting about how it was our last year, how soon we would be leaving Thompson High forever, going off to some other place, no, to some other places.

Grad Week was tons of fun and as the year rolled along, it became more and more obvious that this was different than any other year I had spent at Thompson High. This year, I was getting more involved, I was enjoying every minute. When I would sit in the library with my friends, the conversations always turned to the future. "Where are you going?" we would ask, and "what are you doing?" Everyone's answers were uncertain. There were lots of 'maybes' and 'who knows' and 'ifs' . . . lots and lots of 'ifs.'

Everyone had some dream, something that seemed a little like a plan, but would we make it? Nothing was for sure. Nothing, that is, except what we had already had, our time here together at Thompson High. We had taken that time for granted, until now that it was ending.

Most conversations about the future ended with "Well there's always email. We have to stay in touch" or "But you're staying in town – so it'll be the same number." Or "We'll stay in touch – we have to!" And when we said it, we meant it; we really did want to stay in touch – badly. But none of us knew if we would really be able to after we stopped meeting in the halls, after we stopped bumping into each other at the lockers or in the cafeteria, after the end of this year.

The year rolled along, classes and tests, projects and papers, Christmas break and then exams. And then it began all over again with the new semester – the tests, the papers, the projects, the plans for the end of the year, and beyond.

Every so often, Grad committee announced a fundraiser for grad. The word was that plans for prom sounded promising.

"Any news on where we're having the prom?" Tanya asked. There were two months left before graduation and I was standing in the hallway with a group of friends between classes.

"I heard that they booked a really nice hotel," Monica answered. "Really nice."

"I hope so," Laura said. "With tickets that expensive, it better be nice."

Lisa smiled broadly, "guys – I can't wait for prom night!" She caught my eye and giggled excitedly. I smiled back.

The bell rang and our group dispersed, each of us going to our own class. Laura walked with me down the hall, "Fatima – haven't you told them yet?"

"No, no one knows I might not come. Don't tell, Laura." We stopped at the stairwell for a second. "I might be able to come, I'm not sure. I don't know."

"That'd be awesome," Laura yelled over her shoulder as she headed down the stairs. "Try Fatimah!"

At lunch time, it was more about the prom. We sat outside, letting the May sun warm our faces against the cool wind. My friends were chatty as they ate. I was usually loud, but today, I busied myself with eating. I was listening to everything they said about the prom, trying to picture it. Trying to figure it out.

"I've already got my dress," Lindsay was saying.

"You have?" Hillary's eyes were wide. "We don't even know where it's going to be and you have your dress!"

"That's so Lindsay," Emily muttered, shaking her head.

"Guys, . . . , guys . . ." Anna was yelling from across the circle. I watched her trying to get everyone's attention. All the other girls were involved in one conversation or another. "Hil – lar – y" Anna sang out in a desperate attempt to get her attention. "Hillary, we do know where the prom's going to be."

Most of the chatter stopped. We all looked at Anna, waiting. "It's at the Sheraton."

"No way!" Nancy exclaimed.

"Yes way!" Emily answered.

"Oh this is good," Amy broke into a huge smile. The girls were all talking at once. At first, I tried to listen to all the conversations at the same time, but soon after I gave up. I found myself picturing my friends sitting in a hall in the Sheraton downtown. I wondered what the hall would look like.

"It's a beautiful ballroom," Jamie was saying. "Kelly went to check it out, you know, before they booked it. She was telling me about it. It's really really posh."

"Ooooh," Amy raised her eyebrows.

"Posh is good," Laura added.

Just then Lisa plopped down next to me – her lunch in her hand. "Hey," she smiled.

"How was volleyball?" I asked her, moving over a little to make room for her in the circle.

"Good. Tough. What did I miss here?" she motioned with one hand to our friends. The excitement was obvious in their chatter.

"The prom," I started, "it's going to be in a ballroom at the Sheraton."

"For real?" she grinned. "That's great."

"It is great," Emily confirmed. "I didn't think grad committee would come through. Honestly, they've been so disorganized all year. They haven't done a single thing right."

"Tell me about it," Laura chimed in. "White coveralls? Hello. Blue is tradition."

"Yeah, the way things were going," Emily continued. "I thought we'd end up having prom at Denny's or something."

Laura and I both laughed at the idea, how ridiculous, yet how likely, it was.

"Emily. Girls." Lisa frowned. "Don't talk like that. You don't know how hard it is to be on grad committee and plan all this stuff."

"Well they get their tickets for free – so they better be working for it!" Laura snapped back.

"But why are we mad at them now?" Lisa asked. "Prom's in a ballroom at the Sheraton, right?"

"Ah, girls, lighten up already" Emily shrugged. "It was just a joke, Lisa."

"Has anyone here been to that Sheraton?"Lindsay asked the group loudly. A few people shook their heads.

"You're so funny," Anna said, shaking her head in disbelief. "Why would we go to a hotel here? We live here!"

"Kelly saw it," Jamie said. "And so did Andrew and Robby and Sarah. They say it's awesome – 5 stars! I can't wait!"

"Me neither," several girls echoed.

I glanced around the circle. My friends' faces were glowing with excitement. I glanced at Laura, I wanted to talk to her. She was in the middle of a conversation with Amy and Emily. I waited, but they kept talking. I bumped into Laura, did it so it would look accidental, but she didn't even notice. I turned to Lisa on my other side – she was talking with Jamie, about prom. Didn't matter, I couldn't talk to Lisa anyway. I looked back at Laura, chatting away. I stood up slowly. "Guys, I'm gonna have to go to the library for some research," I said. My explanation fell on deaf ears. I walked away from the circle without so much as a "bye" from anyone – they were all busy, busy talking about prom. At least by the time I had made it up the grass hill to the front doors, Laura had noticed I was gone. She waved at me right before I headed inside. I pretended not to see her.

At the library, I sat at the table with four books open and my pen in hand, a fresh piece of paper in front of me. I read the same line over and over again before I finally let my eyes drift away. I stared at the bookshelves, dazed. Ten, twenty minutes, I don't know. When the bell rang, I snapped out of it. I rushed to gather my things and make it to class on time. In the halls, everyone was talking about prom.

My afternoon classes dragged on –I was in no mood to study. On the bus ride home, I finally let myself think about prom. 'It's not so bad,' I thought. I wanted to go so badly. Very badly. 'Well, why shouldn't I? I mean, this is going to be the last time ever that I can see all my friends.' I let myself ponder this thought, let my mind linger on it. Now I wanted to go even more badly. I pictured my friends, dressed-up and sitting around a table, pictured them sitting there. In my mind I pictured Laura first, then, beside her, Amy. On her other side, that's where I was supposed to be. 'Why not?' I asked myself. 'Why not be there?'

For the rest of the week I tried to answer that question. I found out more and more about prom – where, how, who, what – I asked all the questions.

It sounded like it would be awesome – a night to remember. First we were going to the Sheraton, the grads and our parents, for dinner. The evening would begin at six o'clock. There were going to be large round tables that seat 12 people. We had to tell grad committee ahead of time who we wanted to share our table with, otherwise they would assign us to a table with anyone they wanted.

The program seemed good. First there was the arrival at six o'clock. Then, at 6:30 there was an address by Leah, the grad committee president and another address by our student council president, Pete. Then there was dinner, catered by the Sheraton. After dinner, there would be dancing. That took us until 11 o'clock. After that the party moved to a night club, without the parents.

I ruled out the night club after-party, but that didn't mean that I couldn't go to the prom. The more I thought about it, the more it seemed like a good idea. Parents were invited for dinner at the Sheraton – that definitely meant that things wouldn't get out of hand. And the dancing was no big deal – I just wouldn't dance.

It all settled in my head and, in the end, I was thrilled. I wouldn't have to miss my high school prom after all. I would get a chance to say bye to my friends, to get nostalgic one last time.

On Friday night, I told my parents about prom night, told them about the dinner and that they were invited, told them that I wanted to buy tickets for all three of us. They said we would need to talk more about it – find out more about the dinner. So I told them about the after-party and that I didn't even want to go. (The truth was that some part of me wished I could – but knew I couldn't. There would be too much drinking and dancing.) They said to let them think about it, that we should talk again tomorrow. Didn't they realize that all I had done since the beginning of the week was think about it? I was through thinking – I wanted to decide.

On Saturday, I spent most of my day buried under my books, trying to meet the looming due dates, trying not to think about my mom and dad thinking about prom. In the afternoon, there was knocking on my door – my dad was bringing me a snack.

"I brought you some cookies Fatimah," he said putting the plate down on my desk.

I nodded and gave a quick smile. 'Do you know about prom yet?' I thought. I wanted to ask him. I turned back to my books.

"So, what are you working on?"

"English," I mumbled.

"How's it going?" he asked.

"Okay."

"Good," he turned to leave. "Good luck."

As the door closed behind him my face reddened. I couldn't work. I got up from my desk and walked over to the window. I stared out the window. I thought of Laura and Lisa and Emily. I thought of Hillary and Amanda. I had spent four years with them – four years! I had to go to prom.

It was seven o'clock at night. I was still trying to finish my novel study.

"Fatimah," my mother's voice called up. "Fatimah, it's dinner time."

I stood up and headed into the hall. "I can't Mama," I called back. "I'm not hungry right now and I'm working on English."

My mother appeared at the stairs. "Fatimah, come down for dinner. You've been working all day. Even if you're not hungry – you need a break!"

"But I have to finish this," I protested.

"A half-hour break," she insisted. "It'll help you work better after."

I walked slowly down the stairs. 'Prom, prom, prom,' I thought as I seated myself at the table. 'First snack and now dinner. But never any talk about prom.'

I was hungry. I ate quietly, but my brothers and sisters chatted around me. I resented them. 'They would be mad too,' I told myself, 'if this was their last year of school and they didn't even know if they could say bye to their friends or not!'

When dinner was over, I went back up to my room. I tried to work. I ended up lying down on my bed, staring at the bumps on the ceiling. There was knocking on the door. "Come in," I called. My mom came in and sat on the bed next to me. She patted my hand.

"How's the novel study coming along?"

"Okay," I sighed.

"About prom night, Fatimah," she started.

"Yes – " I interrupted, sitting up suddenly.

"What do you think?" she asked me. "Do you think it's okay to go?"

"Yeah," I answered. "I think so. The parents are going to be there so it's not like people will be – you know – will be –" I didn't know exactly how to say it. My mom looked at me intently, waiting. I realized that she didn't know what I meant. I'd have to explain it. "Okay," I began again. "I think that since parents will be there, then the students are going to act okay. You know? Girlfriends and boyfriends and dates – they're not going to be rude. You know what I mean?"

"I do," she said slowly, "but I'm not sure that parents being there will stop those couples from being inappropriate," she continued. "You know Fatimah, they have a different standard than we do. Their parents might not consider them doing these things in public to be rude. Their parents could actually approve of this and encourage it and be happy that their children are growing up."

My heart sank and my face started heating up. Was this it? Noooooo. Why? I had to go to prom. "But Mama," I protested. "It won't be like that. The dinner is with the parents. It's at the Sheraton. The after-party will be the bad stuff." My mom nodded. The look on her face was so thoughtful, so ready to weigh out the different options. I didn't have that sort of time. Couldn't she see how important this was? Couldn't we bend a few rules? Couldn't I just go?!?

"What about the dinner?" she finally asked.

'The dinner!' I thought. 'What could possibly be wrong with the dinner? Oh no!' I looked at her blankly, my face glum. "The dinner?" I asked quietly.

"Yeah – do you know if they'll be serving alcohol?"

"No." My heart fell. "It's a school event Mama. That's what the after-party is for."

That night I lay in bed trying to sleep, thoughts swimming through my head. Aisha, my sister was fast asleep, her breathing thick. I suddenly felt very jealous – she had nothing to worry about; she wasn't leaving her friends forever. How could I not go to prom? That would be so unfair.

My thoughts swirled around inside my head. I remembered my friends' conversations, remembered my own careful investigation. I had been positive it was okay. Then, one conversation with Mama and it all came crashing down. No, I didn't want high school to end like this. I lay there, thinking, then drawing blanks. It felt like I would never fall asleep.

Monday morning on my way to school, a memory from earlier in the year crept into my head. It stayed there, haunting me. My mother had said over the weekend that the parents being invited didn't mean that couples would behave properly, that parents might not think that public displays of affection were wrong. I had had my doubts. Now, on the bus ride, I was remembering a conversation I had had with my friend Cindy.

"My mom keeps bugging me about getting a boyfriend," she had told me. "She thinks I'm strange because I'm 17 and I'm not dating anyone." I remembered how strange it had sounded then.

Then I remembered another incident this year. It was the Friday before Halloween and everyone was supposed to dress up in costumes for the day. Through the halls, I had seen witches and goblins, fairies and punks with green and pink hair. But I hadn't seen anything more shocking than Mr. Robertson. Mr. Robertson had taught me social studies, gym, and health. He was a fair teacher and a nice guy. He had seemed reasonable, until I had seen him on that day.

Mr. Robertson was a terrible sight in his mini-skirt and tiny Mini-Mouse T-shirt. He had stuffed two big balloons into his shirt and was walking the halls in pink high-heeled sandals. His legs bulged out from under the skirt – too short, too much. His face was painted all sorts of shades with blush, lipstick, and mascara. It was disgusting. It was even more disgusting to see the faces of both teachers and students light up when he was mentioned. When the principal announced over the P.A. system that Mr. Robertson had won "Best Costume for Teachers," he was met with cheers and applause from the whole school.

How could a teacher have thought that something as disgusting as that was just good fun? How could they have voted him best costume?

Was Mama right? No, I really wanted her to be wrong. I wanted to go. I wanted the fact that parents were coming to mean that things would be fine. I got off the bus and walked slowly up the street to my school.

That day at school, I looked everywhere for Leah, the grad committee president, to ask her if there was going to be alcohol at the dinner. I didn't find her anywhere.

The next day, I searched for her again. Monica said that she had seen her. Laura and I combed the halls and the fields for her at lunch. Nothing. "At this rate, I'll never find out," I muttered.

"Fatimah," Laura coaxed, "just buy the tickets. Some people aren't even legal drinking age. They won't be able to drink there."

It was Wednesday and I still hadn't found Leah. I sat inside my chemistry class, glancing over the homework that we were about to take up. From the corner of my eye, I saw Lindsay waving frantically at me from the hallway. I stood up and walked over to Mr. Nelson.

"Can I go to the bathroom?" I asked.

"Class just started."

"I'll be quick."

"You miss what you miss, Fatimah."

I headed out into the hall and walked quickly over to Lindsay. "Leah's in the cafeteria right now," she told me.

"Thanks Lindsay!" I sped down the hallway. Lindsay didn't know why I had wanted to talk to Leah. I wondered, if she had known that I wanted to make sure there was no drinking at the dinner, would she still have hunted me down when she'd seen Leah. I wondered if Lindsay wanted to drink at the dinner.

"There's drinking," I told Laura at lunch. We were sitting alone in an isolated corner of the hallway near the gym. I was slumped over my lunch. I had lost hope.

Laura chewed slowly on her sandwich. "I want you to come," she repeated. She'd already said it six times. I wished I hadn't brought her here so we could eat lunch alone. I wished we were outside with the rest of our friends. I wished there was no prom. "I want you to come to prom, Fatimah," Laura said again. "It's the last time we're seeing each other here in high school. We're gonna be off at different universities next year," she looked up from her lunch now. "You can't not come."

Suddenly, I was angry with Laura. Why was she doing this to me? Why was she making it even harder? She was my best friend – she was supposed to help me out, not make me feel miserable. "Why not, Laura?" I retorted. "Why is this different than all the other dances that I've missed all through high school, huh? Why?"

"Because!" Laura answered. "This is not a dance. This is prom. It's goodbye. It's the last time, Fatimah. Don't you get it? This is supposed to be the best memory that we take with us. And if you don't come, then you won't be part of it. So how's that fair to me?"

The tables had turned somehow and now I was supposed to make Laura feel better. We both felt rotten. The afternoon of classes was terrible. In Spanish class, Cindy and Tanya sat behind me and talked about prom until I wanted to turn around and yell at them. I wanted to yell at the entire class, no, at all the grads. What was wrong with them? Why couldn't they have the stupid dinner without alcohol? They were going to be drinking all night at the after-party. Why the dinner? Why – why did they have to ruin the dinner for me and take away any chance I had of going to my prom?

After school I was slow at my locker. The school halls emptied out around me. When I had finally gathered all my things, I headed down the main hall to the library to drop off some books. "Hey Fatimah," Hillary called. She was standing in the hallway with Anna and Zainab. I headed over slowly. "Have you got your tickets for prom yet?" she asked. I shook my head. "Me neither," she replied.

"I'm buying mine sometime this week," Anna started. "It's just I have to wait to see if my dad and step-mom will be able to come or not. But Zainab beat us all to it."

"Yep," Zainab smiled, "got mine yesterday."

"You're going?" I asked.

"Of course," she said.

"Did you get your parents' tickets too?" Hillary questioned.

"Yep –"

"Where'd you get them from?" Hillary asked.

"The table at lunch," Zainab answered. "Same place that we get the student tickets."

I'd heard enough. "I've gotta get going girls. See you tomorrow." I headed towards the library. How could Zainab be going to prom? And her parents? Does she know that there's going to be alcohol? She's religious. She wears a hijab, for crying out loud!! And she's going to prom. Uuggghh. Nothing made sense, nothing.

That night I didn't tell my parents anything. I couldn't – it was too fresh and painful. The next night I told them about the drinking at the dinner. They nodded quietly and said that it was too bad. But I knew that they hadn't wanted me to go. I went up to my room and threw myself onto the bed. My thoughts took over.

'Why can't I go to prom?' I thought. 'Zainab gets to go. This just isn't fair. This can't be it. But the odds are piled up against me. What can I do? First, the whole thing about how couples will be acting – some couples think that the school halls were made for their private use. They'll be terrible at a ballroom in a hotel, with dancing after. Yeah, of course – the dancing – there's another reason I can't go. Can't I just not dance? Couldn't it be okay for just this one time? Couldn't we make an exception?' I sighed. This was exhausting. 'But the drinking, what could I possibly do about that?' The same thoughts kept surfacing and resurfacing. I lay there for an hour, maybe for two. I fell asleep without doing my homework or setting my alarm clock. When my mom woke me up the next morning, I just couldn't go to school.

"I don't feel up to it, Mama," I mumbled.

"Will you miss anything important?" she asked me.

I shook my head. Nothing important enough.

I moped around the house that Friday. I needed the break – I didn't want to see Laura or anyone else. I didn't want to hear about prom, prom, prom! But nothing I did seemed to make me feel any better.

At noon, I got an idea – I could go if I sat at a table with no drinking. I got excited – I got planning. I made a few rough lists of who might not mind. The number wasn't up to 12 yet, but I would call Laura after school – we would think of enough people!

At 2:30 in the afternoon, the smell of stew crept into my room. I was starving. I finished my game of Minesweeper and went down to the kitchen. Mama was standing at the counter, chopping away at some carrots. Pots were steaming on the stove.

"You look better Fatimah," Mama smiled. "Do you want some stew?"

"Yep – it smells delicious and I'm starved."

She served me a big bowl of steaming stew and put it down in front of me. I dug in. We talked about our plans for next week. We were going to a picnic with a few other families. We talked about what we should bring for dessert. I voted for chocolate fudge brownies and fruit salad.

"Mama," I began cautiously, finally mustering up the spirit to venture talking about the prom again, to share my new solution. "I was thinking, for the prom, that maybe I could still go if I can find a group of people who won't drink. And we can all sit at the table together." I watched her face for a hint of what she thought. Nothing. She put the knife down on the cutting board and took a seat at the table beside me. No. Her answer was going to be no. I looked into my stew.

"Fatimah," my mom began. "You must really want to go to prom."

'Well yeah!' I thought. 'Of course, I really want to go. And that's perfectly normal. It's not normal not to go.'

"Fatimah, we need to look at this a little more objectively. I need you to try to see it for what it is."

"What is it?"

"Well from what you've told me, people are coming as couples, right? Boyfriends and girlfriends?"

"Not all of them. The ones that don't will just bring dates, but they won't be their boyfriends," I explained.

"So you'll be there with people that are out on dates."

"But not all of them. Some people can't find dates – or don't want dates – they just go with friends. Or go solo."

"So a lot of people will be bringing dates," my mom started.

"Well," I interrupted. "We can't say a lot. We don't know how many."

"The default, Fatimah. What's the default?"

I frowned. The default was that they were bringing dates.

"Fatimah," my mom began again. "Let's look at this again. Some people will be brining dates and others won't. Everyone will sit down for dinner and people can order wine then. Since it's a fancy event, Fatimah, most people will."

"Not necessarily," I interrupted again. I knew she was right. Even my friends, who had looked down on drinking before, had started drinking last year. At a fancy dinner in the ballroom at the Sheraton – they would so be drinking, and so would their parents. Why did it have to be like this?

"So you don't think most people will be drinking?" she asked.

I shrugged, "Maybe."

She nodded.

"Some people will be," I said. 'Most, if not everyone,' I thought miserably.

"So after the dinner," Mama continued. "Then it would be dancing for the rest of the time."

"Yes," I conceded, "but the dancing will be on the dance floor and I'll stay at the tables. It's not like I'm going to be in the middle of the dancing or anything."

I paused for a moment. Mama didn't say anything. 'Did I just say that?' I thought. My arguments were getting really lame. 'It's not like I'm going to be in the middle of the dance floor.' What was I thinking? How ridiculous of an excuse is that?

I felt like there was no escape, no way out. First grad committee had cornered me by making prom so impossible to go to, and then my parents, and now I had cornered myself by making those ridiculous arguments. It was over and I had lost. It didn't matter if by some miracle, I found 11 people who wanted to sit at my table and not drink alcohol, there were too many other things. I felt a knot forming in my throat. My eyes welled up. I looked down.

I felt my mother's hand on my shoulder. "Fatimah," she said softly. "Fatimah."

"What? You're right. I won't go. I'll miss my prom. I'll never have that memory and none of my friends will have the memory with me either. All my friends will go off and have a great time and I won't be there." I was crying openly now, staring at my mother, daring her with my eyes to tell me this wasn't important. "I've been there for the last four years, but I don't get to be there for prom night. I don't get to be there to say goodbye." The tears rolled down my wet cheeks. I was out of breath, exhausted, and upset. Mama hugged me tightly. I let her hug me, grudgingly, still angry with her for not agreeing.

That night when my brothers and sisters came home, I distracted myself with them. I didn't want to think about the prom anymore.

It was late. I was looking through magazines with Aisha, trying to help her find pictures for a collage she was making for art class.

"I'm hungry," Aisha whined. We had been working at the collage for three hours now. The floor was covered with magazines and scraps of paper and scissors and unwanted pictures, cut out, at first, because they were needed, then discarded, because we had found better.

"Me too, but this thing's only half done," I motioned to the tentative collage, part of the page empty, the other part crammed with images, competing for a place.

"I know, but I'm bored with it." Aisha lay down on the ground, on scraps and magazines. "I'm totally craving chocolate."

"Mmm . . ." I stood up and pulled her up off the ground. Down in the kitchen, we searched the cupboards and the fridge.

"Nothing," I announced, finishing my half of the kitchen.

"Nooo," Aisha cried out. "I was counting on you, cuz I didn't find any either."

"Go and check Salima's room," I told her. "She's always got something stashed away. Aisha was off in a hurry. When she came back down the stairs, her hands empty, lips pouting, and shaking her head, she found me pouring measured oil into a mixing bowl.

"Fatima . . . ?" she asked.

"Yes . . ." I answered. "Pass me an egg."

"What are you making?" she asked, handing me the egg.

"Brownies. Butter the pan, will you, Aisha?"

"Oh," Aisha' squealed. "Brownies!!"

"Shhh – you'll wake everyone up."

"Brownies!" she squealed again, lower. "Midnight and you're making brownies. You're nuts! I love you – Brownies!"

I laughed, "I'm nuts?" I questioned. Aisha was acting delirious.

Only half the batter made it into the pan. Aisha and I sat in the living room and waited for it to bake. For the first 10 minutes, we were carried by our excitement. After that, our eyelids drooped and we talked nonsense, trying to keep ourselves awake until the brownies were finished. The conversation got shorter, the pauses longer. During one of those pauses, I suddenly remembered the prom, remembered my conversation with Mama this afternoon, remembered my anger and sadness and felt my eyes well up again. 'No,' I thought, 'not again.' But it was too late – I was crying.

"Fatimah, what's wrong?" Aisha asked.

I told her the whole story, told her how angry I was, how upset, told her what I hadn't been able to tell Mama, that it wasn't just the biggest dance of the year, but it was the last time to see my friends, to share a laugh and a story and a memory, that it was the last chance to say bye with class and in style – this was prom – and I was missing it all.

We sat in awkward silence for a few moments afterwards and I started to regret my outpouring of information and emotion.

"Can't you have your own?" Aisha asked, interrupting the silence.

"No!" I exclaimed. "You think I could rent a ballroom at the Sheraton and have a no-drinking, no-dancing prom? You've lost it!"

"That's not what I meant, Fatimah," she started. "It's just, the whole problem is not getting to have that time, right, to get together with your friends and have the time to say goodbye."

"Yeah," I opened the oven and checked the brownies. They were done. I pulled the pan out onto the hot plate.

"You could go out for a fancy dinner with your friends," she suggested.

I looked absent-mindedly at the brownies. "It wouldn't be a prom," I said, "but it would be something."

Aisha cut out a honking chunk of brownie and took a bite. "Aah!" she screamed. "I burnt my tongue! But they're yummy!"

I woke up at 11:30 the next morning with names spewing out of my head. Snatching a piece of scrap paper and a pencil out of the collage mess that lay on the floor, I started the list:

Laura, Sarah Ronald, Monica, Lisa, Anna, Christine – she's not really friends with the rest of them. I hesitated. Wait – doesn't matter – she's my friend – yes: Christine. Alexis and Sarah Black, Amanda, . . . Tammy – I'm not sure . . .

The list was drafted and redrafted. I went through my years at Thompson High. There were people that were my friends, but weren't in my same group – I would invite them. This was about seeing my friends one last time.

Mama and Baba were out. When they came back in the afternoon, I rushed down to tell them my new plan. "And I could ask them all not to drink for that dinner and it would be all girls, and we'd get dressed up and have dinner and have a really great time," I concluded. I had been rambling for 10 minutes now. "What do you think?"

My dad smiled, "Well you sound set – which restaurant?"

"Not sure yet," I said.

"We can go look at a few tomorrow if you want."

My mom patted me on the shoulder, "So this will be your own special dinner."

"Yeah," I replied. "Just to give me a chance to say bye, you know?"

She nodded.

That afternoon, I went with my dad to look at different restaurants. I narrowed it down to two. When I got home I called Laura.

"So what do you think?" I asked her, when I had finished explaining.

"It has to be on the Tuesday," Laura said, "cuz Wednesday I have work, and Thursday my mom needs help at Jody's."

"Okay, Tuesday. But should we go to Leonardo's or Bella's Bistro?"

"You're so into Italian," Laura complained.

"Laura," I warned, "just pick."

"Bella's," Laura said slowly, "it sounds nicer."

"Laura!" I laughed. "You don't pick a restaurant because of its name!"

"I do," Laura declared.

In the end, we settled on Bella's. "Tomorrow, I'm gonna be calling people like crazy all day long," I predicted. "I just hope they can all make it."

"You know what, Fatimah?"

"What?"

"I'm glad you're having this dinner, but it still stinks that you're not coming to prom."

I sighed, long and slow.

Sunday morning I woke up anxious and excited. Today I would call them all and invite them. But what if no one could make it? Worse yet, what if nobody wanted to come? After all, there was no drinking and it was all girls . . .

By Sunday night, I had reached all my friends. The plan had

changed – we were going for lunch on Tuesday – evenings were all booked up already. Only Sarah Ronald said she couldn't make it. She was working and she couldn't get the day off. "But maybe I can drop by for, like, 10 minutes during my break or something. I don't know – I'll try."

On Tuesday morning Nikki called me up. "Fatimah, I was just wondering if I could bring Rob along to the lunch, so you guys could meet him."

Rob was her new boyfriend. I thought I'd explained this whole no guys thing. I wanted Nikki to come. I stumbled on my words. "I uh, well – don't get me wrong Nikki – it's just – um," I paused and took in a deep breath. I tried again. "The thing is Nikki, I don't really go out to hang out with guys, you know? It's against my religion. So I was making this girls only."

"Oh so it's like a girl thing," Nikki said.

"Yeah," I replied. "I mean, no offense to Rob or anything. I'm sure he's a great guy."

"Oh, yeah. Don't worry about it," Nikki assured me. "I'll just tell him it's a girl thing. Anyway – I'll see you at one."

"Yep." I let out a sigh of relief as I hung up the phone.

At the restaurant, they set up a row of tables for my 23 friends and I. Nikki came, even though she couldn't bring Rob, and so did all my other friends. Even Sarah Ronald managed to come for literally 15 minutes. "I wouldn't have missed this, Fatimah, not if I could help it," she told me on her way out. We ate and talked and laughed and snapped pictures and more pictures for two hours. Slowly, the group grew smaller and smaller, with each friend saying bye before she left, hugging and making sure yet again that we had each other's emails, and then hugging again. Smiles and giggles, promises of "I'll call you," orders of "call me", heart-felt thank yous: "Thanks for inviting me Fatimah" and "Thanks for coming", and, of course, soft goodbyes, high-pitched, giggling goodbyes, whispered goodbyes, all filled the room, surrounding us at the moments of parting.

Seven of us lingered until the end. We would go for a walk, we decided. We walked through the downtown streets to the park, took pictures around the fountain and then sat on the ground, letting the grass poke us, letting our minds wander. There we talked about next year, about wheres and whens, about hows that none of us knew. There we shared our dreams and held our memories. We sat in the brilliant sunlight, so much behind us, so much to come, and I savoured it, this moment, neither past nor future, but that precious instant in between.

On the bus ride home, I was happy, nostalgic, and sad. I decided Laura was right – it was a shame that I wasn't going to prom because I would miss out on a special time of being with my friends. 'But,' I thought, 'it would be a much bigger shame if I was going, knowing that it wasn't right.'

The Beholder

IT has long been said that beauty is in the eye of the beholder. But it seems the eye of the beholder has become somewhat harsher of late

A judgmental eye it is, with unattainably high standards

But beauty doesn't seem to be the only thing the beholder holds in his eye

Right and wrong seem to differ from eye to eye as well

Ethics and morality are pushed and pulled in many different directions by many different people.

While journeying through life, we will meet some beholders that we wish to call us beautiful

Others we will simply pass on by, not giving a care for their words of praise and support

Parents, classmates, friends, God – each beholder to his own

No two beholders will ever think us beautiful or even ugly in the same way

And then we will encounter the blinded beholder

The one who never sees us, but judges us still

In this beholder's eye, beauty is relative and ever changing

Varying greatly with the time, place and people it comes with

For the sightless must rely on others to describe the image for them.

The truth is that we will face millions of beholders during our short time on this Earth

But the question is, which beholder will we strive to please?